HELPING YOUR CHILD TO READ

Other How To Books for Family Reference

Applying for Legal Aid
Arranging Insurance
Buying a Personal Computer
Cash from Your Computer
Choosing a Nursing Home
Choosing a Package Holiday
Dealing with a Death in the Family
How to Apply to an Industrial Tribunal
How to be a Local Councillor
How to be an Effective School Governor
How to Claim State Benefits
How to Lose Weight & Keep Fit
How to Make a Wedding Speech
How to Plan a Wedding
How to Raise Funds & Sponsorship
How to Run a Local Campaign
How to Run a Voluntary Group
How to Survive Divorce
How to Take Care of Your Heart
How to Use the Internet
Making a Complaint
Managing Your Personal Finances
Successful Grandparenting
Successful Single Parenting
Taking in Students
Teaching Someone to Drive
Winning Consumer Competitions

Other titles in preparation

The How To Series now contains more than 150 titles in the following categories:

Business Basics
Family Reference
Jobs and Careers
Living and Working Abroad
Student Handbooks
Successful Writing

Please send for a free copy of the latest catalogue for full details (see back cover for address).

FAMILY REFERENCE

HELPING YOUR CHILD TO READ

How to prepare the child of today for the world of tomorrow

Jonathan Myers

BOOKS CAN BE FUN!

HOW CAN THEY POSSIBLY BE? IT'S TOO QUIET IN HERE!

LIBRARY

How To Books

Cartoons by Mike Flanagan

British Library Cataloguing in Publication Data
A catalogue record for this book is available from the British Library.

© Copyright 1996 by Jonathan Myers

First published in 1996 by How To Books Ltd, Plymbridge House,
Estover Road, Plymouth PL6 7PZ, United Kingdom. Tel: (01752) 202301.
Fax: (01752) 202331.

Note: The material contained in this book is set out in good faith for general guidance
and no liability can be accepted for loss or expenses incurred as a result of relying in
particular circumstances on statements made in the book. The laws and regulations are
complex and liable to change, and readers should check the current position with the
relevant authorities before making personal arrangements.

Produced for How To Books by Deer Park Productions.
Typeset by Palimpsest Book Production Ltd, Polmont, Stirlingshire.
Printed and bound by The Cromwell Press Ltd, Broughton Gifford,
Melksham, Wiltshire.

Contents

to actively teach your child or it can be used in a less active manner to enhance and support school work (by, for example, careful choice of appropriate reading material for use at home). The book may also be used as a source of basic information to help you decide when there is a remedial problem that needs attention and what can be done about it. Also looked at are some of the problems faced by particular children, such as dyslexia, that can hinder reading development.

The book often refers to a 'learning session'. This term is used because it is more general than a 'lesson' as children learn under a variety of circumstances: for example, during shopping expeditions or during a bedtime story.

All the advice given is intended in order to allow you to provide extra help to your child. It is not intended to be instead of classroom work in schools.

Jonathan Myers

WHICH IS YOUR CHILD?

Reluctant to read   Keen on computers

                    Not interested in school

Watches too much television   Has learning difficulties

                    Dyslexic

Hyperactive   Enjoys learning

                    Asks questions

Enjoys drawing   Quiet in class

                    Has spelling difficulties

Needs individual attention   Enjoys being read to

                    Gets bored easily

Likes word games   Inquisitive

                    Gifted

Pre-school   At nursery school

                    Twins

Has sight problems   Has hearing problems

                    Attention deficit disorder

1
Deciding How to Help

TAKING CONTROL

First of all, don't think of yourself as an overly concerned parent – if you do that is! It is *your* child we are talking about and every moment is precious. Schools and teachers will come and go but you are the one who has overall responsibility for ensuring that every one of those moments is used to its fullest potential.

Simply watching over your child, as he begins and passes through school life, may be enough. But sometimes, you might need to take an active hand to ensure that your child is really learning – setting time aside to read a story together or do a planned activity. The amount of time that you devote to either overseeing or teaching something will depend on the situation both of your child and of yourself.

But *remember*:

* Be aware of what is going on in your child's life.

If you are aware then you will know when your child's skills are developing correctly. You will also know when something is amiss and action needs to be taken.

Paula wonders if she can be of any real help

'There's really nothing to worry about,' said Mrs Roberts, 'George is doing wonderfully well in class here. You leave it to us. He'll be reading in no time.'

Paula went home thinking that maybe George was doing okay after all and that perhaps she should leave it to the professionals.

'Hi, Paula,' called Mrs Cheng, her neighbour, 'What's up? You look as though you've lost something.'

Paula explained her dilemma and that even if she did help she wasn't sure it was the right thing to do anyway.

'You know,' said Mrs Cheng, 'in another five months George is going to have another teacher in another class. Mrs Roberts' responsibility will have ended. What will you do then if George isn't up to standard? And besides, you can read. What's wrong with reading a story together with George occasionally? It may help and you could enjoy it too.'

Hey Mum, why do I have to learn this reading stuff?

If you think about why we need reading for a few moments, you will probably come up with the usual responses. These include being able to:

- read a story or the newspapers
- send and receive letters and faxes
- read books on a variety of subjects
- read the ingredients on food packaging
- give out medicines according to a prescription
- check a computerised till receipt.

Communicating

All this is obviously true and important but there is something even more basic and that is that we are communicating with each other. It is not just information either. Through the funny squiggles on a piece of paper that make up our language, we are able to tell each other our innermost thoughts and feelings on a multitude of topics. From works on philosophy, economics and cookery to the latest comic strip, all are part of this essentially human desire to convey something of our inner experience to another person.

So, when your child asks why reading is important, remember that:

- The ability to read thoughts, written down, is the closest we can get to another person's mind; whether that person is alive or not.

- To communicate with other people effectively, a child must gain control of the spoken and written word.

Transmitting ideas

Written communication has implications beyond any one particular publication as it is a way of building on the knowledge and work of others. Many scientific breakthroughs have come about in precisely this way; helped by the wealth of scientific knowledge that has been painstakingly recorded in books and journals across the world.

Is my child learning the reading skills he needs to know, at the age he needs to know them?

Remember, you can make a loose estimate of this by comparing your child's level of attainment with what you, yourself, can recall achieving as a child of similar age.

How does my child's reading ability compare with his classmates?

Talk to other parents, talk to the teacher, find out what they think.

Even though I know my child is of normal intelligence, is he easily distracted and lacking the incentive to really latch onto reading?

This is covered more fully in Chapter 6.

Is my child significantly behind to the extent that I feel he has a remedial problem?

Again, this is covered more fully in Chapter 6.

Voicing your concerns
There are sure to be numerous other questions that you may ask yourself such as:

● Should I help my five-year-old with his letters?

● Is it possible to develop my child's interest and skills in reading with some simple tasks or activities, such as reading bedtime stories together?

● Is the school doing all it can to develop adequate reading skills?

● Do I want my child to be ahead of others in his class?

● How does my child compare with children, of the same age, who attend other schools?

● Is my child forging ahead, in reading and other subjects, to the extent that the school is unable to provide enough input to keep him occupied?

In order to answer some of these questions approach the school and ask their advice. It's always useful, too, to talk to other parents – you'll find that many of them have the same concerns.

What all this boils down to, though, is deciding whether to:

(a) Help a little – to develop interest and motivation, or just to get your child going, or even to give him an edge.

(b) Approach the school for more significant help.

(c) Approach the school for help that can dovetail with what you can provide at home.

(d) Seek professional help outside the school.

The majority of children who require a little help are perfectly normal and intelligent youngsters who simply need a slight nudge in the right direction. A little support goes a long way and parents are ideally positioned to provide this support.

TALKING TO THE SCHOOL

It is your right as a parent to know what is happening with your child's education at school. If you approach the school in the correct way the information you want should be easily forthcoming.

Fig. 1. How to approach the school.

Approaching your child's teacher

When you want information first approach the class teacher. Many teachers are around after school and make themselves available for a discussion. It may be advisable to ring in advance if you want to make sure that the teacher will be able to speak to you.

Keep in mind that time is often in short supply and that although a child's school day finishes at around 3.30, a teacher's day may continue for several more hours until curriculum planning, marking, meetings and changing displays have been completed.

Some teachers are available early in the morning or at any other times of the day, but:

- avoid trying to hold a discussion when it is clearly obvious that a lesson is about to start.

Collect your thoughts

Know what you want to say, or what you want to find out, in advance of your discussion. In other words, have your questions ready.

You may just want a progress report and this is fine; most teachers will be glad to let you know exactly how your child is getting on. But don't expect a written report. With all the activities in a teacher's day, there simply isn't the time to do this on an informal basis.

Follow suggestions

Good teachers will welcome help from a parent when a child is beginning to fall behind. Often the teacher will make suggestions, such as reading certain parts of a book by a certain day on a regular basis, and this may be all that is required to get your child back up to standard.

Keep cool

If the teacher will not listen to your reasoned point of view when you have an important concern, then avoid confrontation, if you can, and bring the discussion to an end. The next step is to approach the headteacher.

Mr Edwards goes to see the teacher

The bell had just gone and 32 children all rushed to line up outside class two.

'Miss Singh. Could I speak with you about Dale's reading? He hasn't been getting enough books to keep him occupied and . . .'

'I'm sorry to interrupt you Mr Edwards,' said Miss Singh, ushering the children in, 'but this is really a bad time, as class is about to start.

Perhaps you can come by after school, about 4.15, when I'll be able to give you more attention.'

As Mr Edwards was just about to reply that he was a very busy man, the 33rd member of the class pushed passed him with a sharp elbow to his waist − which tempered what he was about to say.

Mr Edwards gave a slight grunt and rubbed the soreness in his side. 'Um, perhaps I'll come back later after all, when you've got more time.'

Approaching the headteacher

Headteachers can be consulted on a variety of matters to do with your child, or the school in general, and many operate an open-door policy which means at certain times of the day their office door is open and they are available to see people on an informal basis.

Choose a good time

Headteachers are usually very busy at the beginning of the day and besides their administrative duties they may also have assembly − which, when they do not teach any lessons, is an important means of maintaining contact with the children. Although it will vary depending on the individual and the school, mid-morning and early afternoon is usually a slower part of the day for many headteachers.

Making an appointment

If you have a serious concern you can make an appointment through the secretary, who will normally be very helpful. Never be fobbed off, though, by a defensive secretary. Keep your cool but make it clear that an appointment must be made.

Alternatively, you could write a short letter (see Figure 2) and if this doesn't produce a response, after about a week, follow it up with a phonecall.

Headteachers are there to help

Headteachers have overall responsibility for your child and should be understanding and considerate about your concerns. They are there to ensure that your child is taught properly and develops as an individual. As before, it will help if you have thought about what you are going to say and have your questions ready.

Who is above the headteacher

A headteacher is responsible to the governors of the school, who dictate school policy, and they in turn are responsible to the Local Education Authority, in state schools. Never feel, therefore, that the way is barred;

```
                              12 Denton Street
                               East Mulberry
                                     Wrexham
                                    DN4 6JB

                       Tel: 01978 634 7654

Mrs F Boynton
Clifton Primary School
Oak Lane
Wrexham DN9 4KD


Dear Mrs Boynton

Over the last few months, I have become very
concerned about Peter's reading as he has fallen
behind considerably.

I have already spoken to Miss Gould about the
problem but would like to discuss this with
you further, so would you let me know when it
would be convenient to come and see you.


Yours sincerely



Denise Horton
```

Fig. 2. Sample letter to the headteacher.

you always have an alternative to approach in the educational hierarchy if the need should arise.

MASTERING HOW TO TEACH

The most important things you can do to help your child – and not just in reading – are to listen and watch. This is at the heart of all good teaching.

By listening and watching you develop an awareness of:

- What your child already knows about reading and stories – how to hold a book; that stories may start 'Once upon a time' ; the meaning of words on street signs; the ability to identify certain letters.

- What your child needs to know – the skills that need to be developed.

- What help you can provide – sharing stories; letting your child see you reading books and newspapers; teaching specific skills, such as words with an 'oo' sound in them.

Learning to read and reading to learn

Reading and learning go hand in hand. So, learning to read is not just for its own sake – as enjoyable as this is – but also for a purpose.

The greater your child's ability, the greater the chance of your child:

- understanding ideas of increasing sophistication and complexity
- being able to transmit these ideas, through writing or talking, to others.

Without the ability to read properly, a child stands a limited chance of being able to take his place in our increasingly technological society. Mastering the art of good teaching, therefore, is not just about the mechanics of reading but about developing a motivated and informed individual – a well rounded person.

Reading and understanding

Never assume that your child understands a new idea or a concept. One of the most intriguing observations that a parent or teacher can make is that although a child can appear to understand what he has just read, his perception may be at odds with yours. For example, he may perceive a good character in a story as a bad character – and be able to support his opinion with a good reason. This is an opportunity for discussion which can serve to encourage a child and help to develop conceptual skills as well as reasoning ability.

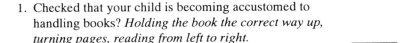

As an individual, a child can have a unique perception of the world – as well as his own agenda!

Things to check
Look at the following list. Have you:

1. Checked that your child is becoming accustomed to handling books? *Holding the book the correct way up, turning pages, reading from left to right.*

2. Found out what reading schemes are used at school? *These are books set at different levels of difficulty. As your child improves he moves on to the next level.*

3. Found out what reading system is used? *The way books are given to children to take home and if you are expected to help in this?*

4. Provided a range of reading material to promote a healthy interest in stories and facts about the world.   _____

5. Answered your child's questions with helpful explanations as well as creating discussion?   _____

6. Made sure that your child sees you reading and enjoying books and stories?   _____

Advantages of teaching your child

As a parent who wants to be involved with your child's education, you are uniquely placed as an educator because:

- You have already taught your child many things including much of the language she speaks.

- You know your child and her foibles better than anyone else and know best how to motivate her.

- You have a long-term interest in her welfare, educational and otherwise.

- You can gear what you do to your child's needs and personality in a way that most schools simply don't have the time to do.

- If you do it right, you can strengthen your relationship with her and create enjoyable moments that will be remembered down through the years.

- By helping your child learn to read at a very young age, the door to the wonderful world of literature will be opened.

- Access to the wealth of book-based knowledge is likely to be gained quicker and your child will start to learn many things about the world around her.

- As your child develops, she will be more likely to seek information for herself, on her own initiative, using her new-found reading skills.

- By you providing feedback and direction to your questioning child, at the appropriate time, the whole educational process is speeded up.

Helping your child to learn to read, therefore, has implications beyond reading itself, entering into many other areas of knowledge.

You are likely to find that you don't actually need to do a great deal to keep the ball rolling, as once you start helping out this will begin to impact on school work in a positive manner.

Disadvantages of teaching your child

Although many parents have good intentions, they may not, unfortunately, be the best people to teach their own children specific skills. Sometimes this is because:

- The relationship is extremely intense and when a child makes a mistake it is taken almost as a personal slant by the parent.

One reason for this is that some parents find it difficult to accept that their offspring, to whom they have given life and nurtured, cannot understand something that they themselves find straightforward. If you are the type of parent who gets easily exasperated with your child, in this manner, then attempting to teach her may not provide the rewards that you had hoped for. This doesn't mean that you can't change, but it does mean that you first have to become aware that you have this type of temperament.

Having patience with your child's mistakes is the key to successful learning, without which your efforts are likely to be counterproductive. The last thing that you want to do is switch your child's motivation off, so that doing any sort of learning activity becomes a chore and something to be avoided.

Overcoming your child's barrier

On occasion, even with a strong positive relationship with your child, she may still not want to read or do an activity with you – and she might try all sorts of excuses to get out of it. This may be because she feels, consciously or subconsciously, that:

- She doesn't want to let you down by failing in her attempts to learn.

Sometimes, this is a result of lack of confidence which may originate in:

(a) Previous unsuccessful tries.

(b) Attempts to hide her lack of knowledge because she believes that she should know more and doesn't want to make you angry by you finding out how little she really knows.

In cases like these, trying to teach your child yourself may not prove feasible and you could make matters worse if you force it. These are situations where you should approach the school or seek outside specialist help as problems can develop to a point where school work is significantly affected.

Teaching the right skills

Assuming that your temperament is suitable, and your child enjoys doing activities with you, then any difficulties that occur will be to do with the content of your teaching and how you have structured it. An extreme example would be if you tried to teach the spellings of some large complex words when your child is still having trouble at school with letter identification. In this case, you are likely to confuse your child and create a worse problem than already exists. You may also get a phonecall from the class teacher — who may have been giving special attention to the letter problem — asking what you've been up to!

Doing better than school

It could be that you are in a situation where you are doing all the right things to provide some extra help in reading and it is indeed working. Your child is making leaps and bounds at school. However, when the teacher finds out why your child is progressing at a faster rate, she feels threatened and gives you a great deal of flak. It is a difficult position to be in but, by approaching the school appropriately, it can be dealt with — it must be dealt with. Otherwise, your child will revert to his previous rate of educational progression.

MAKING LEARNING FUN

How to make learning **fun** is the sixty-four thousand dollar question. If we all knew the answer, it would make the whole process of education much easier for many children. Although, what is fun for one child may be agony for another!

Setting guidelines

What we can do, though, is set some **guidelines**. Keep these in mind as you progress through this book. All the points in this list show that you value your child's efforts and transmit a sense of motivation.

1. Be firm but fair.

2. Be patient with your child.

3. Always give plenty of praise and encouragement – even for mistakes.

4. Talk to your child – communicate.

5. Use a variety of books and materials to provide educational stimulation.

6. Keep interest high by not spending too much time on any one activity but changing to a different activity.

7. Be aware of learning opportunities in different things that you do – and that your child does – and in different locations.

8. Know when to stop – be aware of when your child has had enough for one day.

9. Be aware of, and take an interest in, what's going on in your child's life.

10. Show that you are enjoying yourself when you're helping your child.

CASE STUDIES

Throughout the following chapters, we will follow the progress of three sets of characters as they are faced with situations that can affect education and reading development.

Mary and Sophie

Mary is married and in her late 30s. Her husband, Frank, is an engineer and spends much of his time working away from home, in the North Sea oil fields. Mary is a busy manager in a women's clothes shop and spends most of the rest of her time looking after her two daughters, Sophie, aged five and Polly, aged 14.

Sophie is intelligent and at an age when she is beginning to become an individual with definite likes and dislikes. Mary sometimes feels slightly guilty about not having taken a greater interest in Polly's education when she was younger. She doesn't want to make the same mistake with Sophie and knows that with the right kind of help, Sophie will succeed well in life.

Mary is not sure whether Sophie is getting all the right help from her school. But Mary's time always seems to be taken up with something – her job, her friends, her family, getting Sophie washed, dressed or fed – and she's not sure whether she can have a real impact on Sophie's education anyway; as though educated to degree level, she feels that the world has changed considerably since she finished her education.

Tracy and Sam

Tracy is a young, single mother to six-year-old Sam. Although highly intelligent, Tracy has had a limited education due to poor schooling. She now works as a secretary in an office supply company.

Sam means a great deal to Tracy and she is willing to devote a significant part of her time and money to further his education and give him the best possible start in life. Tracy believes that Sam is getting a good education at school but wants to do more for him.

Bill and Kevin

Bill is a carpenter and is in the process of starting his own business with a builder friend. He is married to Anne. Their son, Kevin, is seven years old and does averagely at school. Although a little abrupt sometimes, Bill is a kind and good-hearted person.

Bill left school after doing well in his A-Levels, particularly in maths for which he has a natural flair. Bill is happy in his work, as he is doing what he enjoys, and both he and Anne want Kevin to be in a similar position. That is, to be able to choose what to do in later life and have the education to achieve it.

POINTS FOR DISCUSSION

1. Whether you decide to help actively with your child's reading or not, why it is useful to speak to the class teacher? How would you make your approach? What would you do if you found this unhelpful?

2. What do you think are the main characteristics of good teaching? Are they applicable to class teachers as well as parents who want to help? How might you use these characteristics in your own approach?

3. Why is reading of vital importance in today's technological world?

that letter and it must be at the beginning of the word. Then, I'll tell you what the whole word is.'

'Okay, Mummy. I know what a 'cuh' is,' said Amy, becoming silent and keen eyed.

Kate and Amy went round further to complete the shopping. At reduced intervals, Amy happily reported seeing a 'cuh' on packets of cake, coffee, crackers, cream and more cornflakes.

How much time do you have?

Time, during which you actually have contact with your child – or can change your routine to include your child – is vitally important. Besides anything else, including the development of reading skills, contact time is needed in order to promote a healthy relationship.

When you look at the list below, you may think that you couldn't possibly find time during some of these daily activities, as your child would just run around, be difficult to control or be totally uninterested – and you want to get the job done as easily and as quickly as possible. There is always that possibility but it is often found that once children are included in a task with an adult, their behaviour begins to change for the better.

Place a tick by each of the daily activities during which you could reasonably teach something using a simple learning activity or game.

For each of these daily activities ticked, write down the number of minutes that you think you could find.

Daily activity	✓or X	*Mins*
Journeys to and from school	_____	_____
Shopping trips	_____	_____
Outings	_____	_____
Sorting clothes or food	_____	_____
Meal preparation	_____	_____
Mealtimes	_____	_____
After supper	_____	_____
Bedtime	_____	_____
Other household tasks	_____	_____
Free time	_____	_____

How often can learning sessions take place?

If you can devote sufficient time for more than two sessions a week, all the better. But bear in mind that even when children are not involved in a specific learning activity, provided there is some continuity, their minds are still working and they are integrating previously learnt information. So, don't overdo it and think that every spare moment must be used.

Theoretically, if there are seven days in a week then all are accessible for use. However, keep in mind that:

1. An adult would dislike working every single day and a child should not be expected to either – which is a good reason for a five-day school or working week.

2. A parent is foremost a parent and generally not a trained school-teacher, so that planning a formal or informal session for every day can be time-consuming and difficult – although good workbooks are available to help you.

3. It might prove counterproductive as your child might tire of the sessions that much faster, unless they are always fresh and exciting.

Modifying your approach

For most children three or four sessions a week is the maximum necessary and sometimes this amount needs to be worked up to over a period of weeks. Don't be afraid to try different combinations of days and times. Each child is an individual and it is often useful to experiment in order to find out what works best for them. The following are two suggestions.

● A pleasant way for a young child to receive greater input is to have a session approximately every other day. These sessions should include enjoyable and fun activities, bedtime stories, as well as informal activities. In this way your child won't even be aware that your intention is to teach him something of importance. It will just be a time to look forward to.

● For some older children and those who require stronger input because they forget quicker, you might find it beneficial to have a session two days running, then a break and then either one or two days again.

put a great deal of thought into what you are going to do.

If you have decided to read a story together, with your child clearly identifying the word 'I' every time it appears in the text, then you have:

- a well defined aim
- a high degree of parent input, as you will be doing most of the reading.

Now think of ways of identifying other one letter words, such as 'a', so that you are planning ahead and beginning to structure your approach.

Next, you need to decide on the setting for the activity:

- It could be as a bedtime story, in a comfortable chair together, or at a table sitting next to one another.

Sitting at a table is like your child sitting at a desk in school and so has a greater formality about it. However, the activities that you choose will often dictate the degree of formality of the learning session. So, for example, if you decide to do an activity with drawing, you will most likely use a table because it has a firm base.

Balancing your act

When it come to *how* you present an activity, as opposed to the setting, the best type of activities tend to have elements of both formality and informality about them. Getting the balance correct is difficult, even for experienced teachers, but if you manage it, you will be using your time together more constructively. After all, you are not conducting an exam but neither do you want your child running around the room when you have planned an important activity. You should attempt to make the session informal enough so as to allow your child flexibility to learn by experiment but formal enough so that your aim is achieved. This takes a little thought but the key is to make it interesting and fun – for both of you.

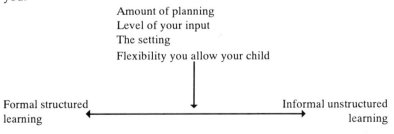

Fig. 3. Getting the balance right.

Bedtime stories are fun for adults too!

Curl up with a good book together with your child and you not only help to develop basic reading skills but you also give your relationship a chance to grow and become strong.

A golden opportunity

Bedtime stories are used at the time of the day when things are winding down and parents are looking forward to a quiet evening. But don't think of it as simply a method of settling a child before they go to sleep and you can go and relax because it is quality time if used correctly.

Pleasant surroundings

When you read a story together, it can be enhanced by the setting. This can include dimmed lights, a soft bed and pillows, and your close proximity. Don't sit in a chair on the other side of the room but get as close as possible, so that your child feels safe, loved and included in the storytelling activity.

A setting like this will help to bring the end of the day to a comfortable finish for your child. It may also do the same for you − helping to calm you after a busy day. Don't worry if you drop off to sleep next to your child − it helps to strengthen your relationship.

Supporting imagination

Ten to 15 minutes spent telling a fairy tale or another type of story that you have specially chosen will begin to open your child's mind to the wonder of stories. It will help to develop their imagination and whet their appetite for more. You might find that your child begins to tell you what happens in the story − they may have heard it before or they may be making it up. This is good as it is a springboard from which powers of expression are developed. The ability to relate an episode or event in a person's own words is an important skill. It touches on powers of observation and understanding; with broadened imagination it can develop into sophisticated storytelling ability.

Sharing the story

If your child wants to participate when you are telling a story, then unless you have a reason, encourage it. Always try to look at an activity from your child's point of view − try and understand what *she* needs from the learning process.

You can tell a story in a more active manner by pointing out and identifying certain letters or words, or you might ask a question like, 'What do you think happens next?' Discuss it for a few moments then move on.

Remember that balance is important. Sometimes it is good to have your child actively participating. While at other times, a more one-way approach, with you telling the story and your child simply listening, is equally useful.

Children like to hear stories again and again and ...

The opportunity to 'practise' some simple emotions, in an enjoyable way, is just too tempting for young children to miss. So they like the familiarity of a story they have heard before. They know the lines, they know the cues, they know when to be happy and when to be sad. Just watch their faces contort as the interesting parts are read. For them, it is all about the expectation involved.

Using variety

As good as it is to tell a story several times or more, you do not want your child to become like the man who read a book and enjoyed it so much that he believed no other book could ever compare. So he never read another book! Make sure that you expose your child to a good spread of stories that have different styles and different storylines.

A new slant to an old story!

Keeping control
Retelling a story is fine but if your child asks repeatedly, on the same occasion, it may be a way of avoiding going to sleep. This is a difficulty that can vary in severity. An extreme example is the child who cries incessantly or bounces up and down on the bed as soon as the parent stops reading. In cases like this the advice of a child psychologist can be sought for a regime to get things back to normal. In the majority of non-severe instances, dealing with the problem is by being pleasant but firm — establishing your authority so that your child knows that if they are good, and go to sleep straight away, then maybe tomorrow night you'll read the story again.

Creating desire
Always leave a story at a high point — a really exciting bit! You will probably get a response such as, 'Aw, but I wanna know what happens?' Your child might even try to turn the page over to peek at the pictures. Be kind but firm. That's the time to close the book, say goodnight, turn the light out and leave the room. As they say in show-biz: 'Always leave them wanting more!'

Things to check ✓

1. Is your child old enough to learn what you want to teach? _____

2. Are you having enough learning sessions together? _____

3. Are you using a mixture of formal and informal activities? _____

4. Have you read a bedtime story together in a comfortable setting? _____

5. Have you made sure there are no distractions, like background TV noise? _____

6. Do you leave stories at a high point to promote interest and excitement? _____

Repeating activities
Children often find pleasure in what has become familiar to them: an object, toy or certain task. These things can easily become part of a child's world because they have gained a degree of mastery over them and feel a

type of ownership. Parents know full well the implications of removing a well loved teddy but they may also hear, on occasion, the plaintive cry: 'But you let me do it before!'

Building on knowledge
The fact that children like to do tasks that they have done before is useful because you can harness their interest in order to refine their skills. After an interval of a session or two you can return to a previous activity. Your child may say: 'Oh, I know how to do this,' at which point you've gained their attention and can proceed.

Activities to which this type of approach is applicable might be a letter game, such as pointing to a particular letter every time it appears on a page of text, or locating a specific letter in a pile of letter cards.

Keeping changes simple
It is also useful to repeat an activity because there are only a finite number of available activities to choose from and you will want to make the most of them. Of course, for added interest you can change an aspect of the activity. For example, instead of looking for one letter in a pile of letter cards, you could instruct your child to look for two at a time such as 'f' and 'l'. You could then show him some simple words that could be made with these *eg* flip, flop and flap. Several sessions later you can return to this activity for a review and later build on it by looking for other letters or letter combinations.

Laura makes the link

For several weeks, Steven had been spending ten minutes every few days with five-year-old Laura, helping her with her letters. Laura now knew how to spell simple words, like 'on' and 'cat', using letter cards. But sometimes when Steven asked Laura for a different word she seemed to get confused and would stare at the letters. Steven wondered what else he could do. He needed to do something that would be a bridge and provide the link that Laura would respond to. Then it came to him. 'Laura,' he said, 'spell 'cat'.'

'That's easy, Daddy.' Laura answered as she formed the word on the table in front of them.

'Now, take the first letter away. What do you get?'

'At,' said Laura, with a pleased smile spreading across her face.

'Now, find a 'muh' in the pile of cards and place it in front of the word 'at'.'

'Okay.'

'What do you get?'

Laura thought for a moment, then happily answered, 'mat'.

'Correct,' replied her father excitedly. 'Let's try another one.'

Over the next few minutes, Laura successfully made the words: 'sat', 'fat', 'rat' 'bat' and 'hat'.

Steven looked on enthusiastically at his daughter. 'See? Just by changing one letter we can get a whole new word.'

The next session they tried the same idea with the word 'it'.

Stop! I can't take any more! — when to stop a learning session

Young children tire easily and the last thing you want is to make learning oppressive. You can always return to an activity another time.

Stop if you see your child:

- yawn repeatedly
- start playing with something that catches his attention.

With many children though, especially as they get a little older, yawning tends to signify boredom or the end of interest in a particular task, rather than tiredness. So, either stop or move onto another different activity.

Be aware of when you're becoming boring. When you see a glazed expression that's the time to stop!

Feeling ill

If a child is unwell, never force them to learn – it is unlikely that they will be able to give their best. However, for minor ailments, such as coughs and colds which need to run their course, light activities can often take children's minds off how they feel. A drawing exercise or a good story read to them can prove beneficial under these circumstances. If nothing else they may tire faster and be able to sleep off their ailment that much quicker.

Don't overdo it

The minimum time required for a learning session is around ten minutes and sometimes a little less for storytelling. However, the maximum session length is around 35 to 45 minutes due to a child's attention span. Certainly, in this time period you could do more than one activity with your child – two or even three activities is quite feasible. After a while you will be able to gauge your child's concentration threshold for different activities and tailor the learning session accordingly. Aim to keep interest high by changing to another exciting activity before your child has a chance to become bored.

At a session length of more than 45 minutes it is inevitable that concentration will be lost. If you consider that many secondary schools use a lesson of this length then it makes sense to use somewhat less, or build up to this length, for a younger child who is having individual attention from you. For most children, it is likely to be counterproductive to have a session longer than this; although to a large extent, it depends on the individual child, his age and his maturity.

Taking the lead

If you have decided that you want to do a particular activity, don't get put off by excuses or yawning and stop, when really your child just wants to watch his favourite TV programme or play his computer game – as important as these can be.

Teachers who tutor at the homes of their pupils encounter cases of crying usually because a child is unwell or – more commonly – because a video film has been interrupted!

WHERE TO LEARN TOGETHER

Obvious places for learning together include:

• your child's bedroom for bedtime stories

- a big, comfortable armchair
- a clean, kitchen table.

Creating a learning area

As your child progresses in learning, you may both feel the need to carry out some of your sessions in a particular area of your home. This may be a simple matter of practicality. For example, you might want to keep books and materials in a place that is near to hand when you learn together or you might want to use a desk for some writing tasks as it is sturdy and you can keep pencils and paper in it. If your child has his own room with a desk or small table, all the better.

Wherever you choose, though, the area should:

(a) have a solid, sturdy surface on which to work
(b) be relatively quiet – away from TVs and radios
(c) not be too hot or too cold
(d) be fairly well ventilated but not draughty
(e) be well lit but not so bright that light is reflected uncomfortably from the pages of books or papers
(f) have materials and books easily accessible
(g) have a comfortable seat for your child to sit on.

The seat and work surface heights should be correctly positioned so that your child is not having to stretch up from a low seat or bend over to a low surface. There should also be enough room for you to sit next to him.

Decorating the learning area

Once you have used the learning area for a while, your child will have produced some fine work; perhaps a drawing based on a story you have read together. Pick some of the best and display it around the learning area – use only sticking materials that won't damage the walls! This type of feedback demonstrates that you value your child's work and is a good motivator. It also brightens the learning area.

WHAT TO LEARN TOGETHER

A wide variety of material can be used and it really boils down to how interesting you make it. Often, with a little thought, the same material can be used in different ways – so you don't need a different book or game for every different activity.

The eagerness with which you approach the activity will be transmitted to your child. The key here is to choose anything that will enhance your child's reading ability and general education in an enjoyable way. Chapter 4 discusses in detail how to choose appropriate material for your child at the right level.

Your child's current needs will dictate your choice. But then you must consider what you want to achieve from the material and what your goals are. This will help you decide what you learn together.

Do you want to:

(a) Increase ability to identify letters.
(b) Help to tell the difference between big letters and small letters.
(c) Increase ability to identify words.
(d) Develop ability to read groups of letters, such as 'oo' and 'ea' or 'ing'.
(e) Increase reading fluency.
(f) Develop interest in a variety of traditional and modern stories.
(g) Help with specific problems outlined by the class teacher.
(h) Develop awareness of the surrounding world through non-fiction, such as space or road safety.
(i) Develop creativity in storytelling.

Available material that you may use includes:

- Any good book or story that you have specially chosen – for reading together or for practising letters or words.
- Poems and rhymes.
- Activity books (bought).
- Activities that you have prepared at home.
- Material sent home from school.

Planning for action

In the table in Figure 4, some of the aims and activities to do have been filled in as an example. Try writing in the blank spaces what is appropriate for your child's needs.

Making stories and rhymes active

Here are a selection of activities that you can use with beginners from about four years of age.

Session	Aims	Activities to do
1	identify 'oo' sound	pointing when reading
2	learn about ships	picture book about ships
3	identify 'oo' sound	noticing 'oo' in shop windows
4	consolidate 'oo' sound	drawing pictures with 'oo'
5	identify 'sh' sound	saying words beginning with 'sh'
6		
7		
8		
9		
10		

Fig. 4. Aims and activities to do.

Fingering

Make sure that your child can see the text clearly as you read along the line. Point to the word as you read it. Read slowly and distinctly so that your child begins to get a feel for the break between words. Watch your child and when she begins to scan as you move your finger, let her put her hand on your finger. Encourage your child to follow where you lead as you speed up a little or slow down along the line.

During another activity, let your child move *your finger*, using it like a pointer, along the line as you read – you might have to cheat a little initially! When she can do this, the next stage is to let your child point by herself and move her own finger as you read the text. It can be quite hard for some children to keep their finger moving steadily and it might slip to another line; if this happens gently move it back into position.

This activity can be the source of some amusement as your child is not reading herself yet but controlling your reading. She can stop moving her finger forcing you to stop reading – don't give in till she starts moving again! She can also speed up or slow down – where you can sound like a tape recorder being played at the wrong speed!

Identifying letters

When you are reading the text, with your child looking at the page, and you come across a letter, such as 't' or 'd', point it out and say what sound it makes. If necessary, take time to actually look at the letter saying which bit is curly, which bit is round, which bit is long and straight or which bit has a tail. The next time you see the letter, pause and ask the question: 'Do you remember what the sound was?' or 'I've forgotten what that letter is. Can you tell me what sound it makes?' When you have the correct response, give plenty of praise saying something like, 'Well done!' (or 'A very good try!' if it wasn't correct). Then carry on reading the story.

Avoid pointing out similar looking letters, such as 'b' and 'd', close together as this can be confusing.

Note that it is highly important to give the sound of the letter as opposed to the name of the letter. A child can put sounds together like building blocks to ultimately form words but he cannot do this with only the names of letters.

An easy way to start on letter identification is to point out words of one letter, such as 'I' and 'a'. The fact that these letters are sounded as they are named can be explained by stating that when letters are on their own they sometimes have a different sound.

Identifying words
Start with one letter words, as mentioned above, then move on to two letter words, such as 'on, 'so' and 'to'. If you have pointed one of these out a few times then it should stick in your child's mind. If it doesn't, simply remind him patiently until it does. Again, always use plenty of praise, even for errors, as it provides motivation.

When it comes to pointing out larger words you may first need to teach that combinations of letters make certain distinct sounds. One of the simplest is a 'th' sound but you can also point out double letter combinations, such as 'oo' and 'ee', to start out with. These are useful as they appear in simple words like 'zoo' and 'feed'.

If your child knows how to do all this then you can move onto other combinations of letters, such as 'br' in *broom*, 'fl' as in *fly*, or 'sl' in *sleep*. Your intention here is not that your child should be able to say the whole word, although this will come with repetition, but that he should be able to identify a specific part of the word — you then give the full reading.

With repetition certain words will stick in your child's mind even though they may not be able to fully identify all the constituent sounds. What is happening is that they are recognising the word as a whole. They are much more likely to do this if the word means something to them. So, be on the lookout for words like 'dog' and 'cat' or 'mummy' and 'ball'.

Missing words
Once your child has a limited reading vocabulary then you will be able to expect greater participation on his part.

As you are reading a line of text pause at a simple word and ask what it is – tell him the answer if necessary. Explain that you are going to stop the next time the same word appears and he can say, as loud as he can, what the word is – if you find it getting too noisy then change to saying it as quietly as he can or saying it in a normal voice.

As you progress with this you can add more words from the text. To make it more interesting you can ask him to use different types of voices for the various words, such as squeaky ones or low pitched ones – these are good for animal words.

Missing lines

If the text is easy enough then you can alternate reading lines with your child. This can be quite heavy going for many children. So, only do it for a bit, or until your child gets used to it, then carry on reading all the text yourself for a while.

When more proficiency is gained, you can move on to alternating reading pages together in the same way.

Talking about the story

Don't just concentrate on the mechanics of reading but aim to develop an appreciation of the story. Discuss, with your child, the pictures that may be present, with attention to how they relate to the story. Talk about the characters – what they might be going to do next or whether they're nice or horrible. Ask for your child's opinion as to whether a character's actions are the correct ones – or you might phrase it differently asking whether *she* would have done the same thing in those circumstances. You may be quite surprised to find out the depth of opinion a six-year-old can hold.

When discussing things with your child, keep your language simple but avoid talking down to her.

CASE STUDIES

Mary and Sophie – a twice weekly bedtime story

It had been a long, hard day and just as Mary was about to flop down in an armchair, before making supper and putting Sophie to bed, the phone rang. It was Sophie's teacher, Mrs Briggs.

Mary listened as Mrs Briggs told her that although Sophie was a lovely, bright girl, who was undeniably intelligent, she was falling behind in her school work and that a reason for this was that she was a poor reader.

Children's understanding can often surprise adults.

Mary's first reaction was annoyance. 'Why,' she asked, 'wasn't the school doing more?' And why, she thought, wasn't the teacher doing more?

Mrs Briggs explained that all the children in the class received the same input and, in fact, those children like Sophie, who needed greater attention, had the benefit of a specialist teacher as well as regular reading sessions with volunteer class helpers. What Sophie needed was experience and practice to bring her up to standard – she already had many of the pieces, appropriate for her age, that form the backbone of good reading ability. 'Would it be possible,' Mrs Briggs suggested to Mary, 'to read a little at home with Sophie?'

Initially, Mary balked at the idea. She hadn't the time – or the energy, for that matter. But then Mary considered that Sophie needed the opportunity to succeed and maybe she had been neglecting her daughter's education a bit. The discussion continued for a while with Mary looking for ways to help Sophie that would not involve her directly. Mrs Briggs then said that really all that was required in terms of commitment was around ten minutes twice a week. Mary was silent as the penny dropped that, for so little input on her part, so much could be gained.

A few days later, Mary made the effort to read a story for a few minutes with Sophie after putting her to bed. Very soon, it became a regular feature of the time Mary and Sophie spent together; which they both thoroughly enjoyed and looked forward to. Within a few weeks, Sophie became more interested in the things she read and more competent with letter sounds she previously had trouble with. In addition, Sophie's school work improved dramatically.

Tracy makes a learning corner for Sam

Tracy was feeling pleased with herself. She had done two informal sessions with Sam the previous week – some sequencing, putting all the shirts in the shirt pile, which led on to finding things in the kitchen cupboard beginning with the letter 's'. A few days later, Sam brought home from school a picture he had drawn – it showed Sam's home and was covered with the letter 's' and every time Sam saw the letter he would say what it was.

To take this further and spend a few minutes sitting with Sam, Tracy decided to make an area of the lounge in her flat into a learning corner. Moving a little coffee table and two comfortable chairs was all that was needed. And after obtaining some paper, pencils, crayons and a pencil case to store them, they were ready to try the learning corner out. Their first session produced a brightly coloured picture of a cat, beautifully patterned all over with the letter 'c' and the name 'Sam' boldly written across the top. Tracy liked it so much, she had it framed the next day.

Bill gets boring!

Over the previous few weeks, Bill had been doing well teaching Kevin some letters and reading with him. One day Bill decided to try some non-fiction material about cars. The book was extremely interesting and very soon Bill became totally engrossed himself. Kevin listened for a while as Bill went into a lengthy discourse about why some classic cars were far better than modern cars. Within several minutes Bill was off, talking about gear ratios, manifolds, carburettors and spark plugs – there was no stopping him. Kevin's head sunk lower and lower as the words passed him by without making any impression, except a desire to go and hide in his bed until the onslaught had finished.

Finally, Bill said, 'Isn't that really interesting, Kevin?'

'Yes,' croaked Kevin, with a strained voice and a glazed expression!

POINTS FOR DISCUSSION

1. Why do you think it's useful to have more than one learning session a week, whether formal or informal?

2. Why is it important to convey a sense of eagerness when you teach your child?

3. Stories can be told in a one-way style, with you telling it and your child listening, or your child can participate actively. What is the value of both approaches?

3
Learning with Your Child

BEGINNING WITH LETTERS AND SOUNDS

Begin at the beginning. The letters and the sounds they make are strongly connected and the activities you do should reflect this in a simple manner.

You could start with an informal activity (see Chapter 2) or a game that identifies letters and links them to particular objects (see page 59: Learning letters with simple ideas and games).

Essentially, these give a child the knowledge to state that:

- an 'a' (ah) is for an apple
- a 'b' (buh) is for a bat
- a 'c' (cuh) is for a cat, and so on.

Sounds first
Because letters are like building blocks, it's important to teach the sounds of letters before their names. Similarly, teach lower-case letters before upper-case letters.

Remember:

- It's 'ah' for apple and not 'a' even if you feel a little silly saying it!

Starting off the right way
The teaching of the sounds of small letters first cannot be overstated. This is the stage at which many children begin to do badly in reading at school. They start to identify letters by a mixture of upper- and lower-case sounds and then cannot combine them to form words.

Remember that what you are attempting to do, in effect, is teach two different alphabets.

a b c d e f g h i j . . .

A B C D E F G H I J . . .

So:

- First introduce small letters and their sounds and then move on to big letters and their sounds – once your child has a rudimentary grasp of the basic sounds. It makes sense to do it this way as small letters are far more common in a page of text.

Someone got there before you

'But Mum, Nurun told me it's an "ay" and he knows 'cause his dad's a teacher.'

'Yes I know dear,' said Beth, wondering how she could convince Richard that she did know what she was talking about, even if she felt as though she was losing her confidence.

'It really is, Mum, really. It's an "ay" and anyway, I stopped saying it the baby way in Mrs Platt's class!'

'I know you did and you're quite right but sometimes it's useful to say it as an "ah". Can you think of a reason why?'

'Uh, no.'

'Well, let me show you an interesting game that we can play,' replied Beth, as she rearranged the letter cards.

Simple ways to introduce upper-case letters

The following are two ideas for introducing upper-case letters so that your child learns to differentiate between the two forms of the alphabet.

1. Point out that names always start with them. Form a simple activity around this idea by having your child identify the names of family members from a long list of names that you have formulated earlier.

2. Link them with their lower case counterparts. A simple method of doing this is by writing them, small, in the corner of a letter card. You can make letter cards quite easily by writing, in a simple script, all the lower case letters of the alphabet on six centimetre by four centimetre pieces of paper. When the letter cards are used for activities both upper and lower-case letters will be observable by your child.

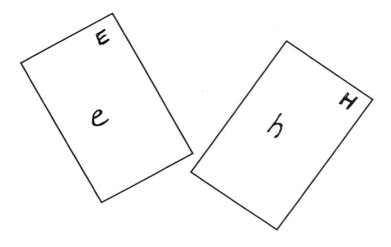

Fig. 5. Letter cards.

Making reading mean something

Whatever non-book activities you do always back it up with plenty of
stories so that your child has a chance to understand how the letters are
used in reality.

Should the alphabet be taught?

The traditional approach was to have school children chanting the alphabet. Educationalists moved away from this approach because it was felt
that knowledge of the letters would be far better developed if children
were motivated with stories and reading that were of greater interest to
them. To some extent this is true but like most things in life balance is
important.

So, keep in mind that:

- You don't need to teach the whole alphabet in sequence first but you
  do need to teach some letters before your child's motivation and natural learning ability can get started.

But this doesn't mean that you can't refer to the whole alphabet. There
are many colourful books and wall friezes, easily obtainable, to help you.
These have the alphabet printed with accompanying pictures that demonstrate what the letter can be used for.

Some letters are difficult

It is fairly common for young children to have problems with certain letters such as:

- confusing 'u' and 'y'
- saying 'v' for 'f'
- forgetting 'x' and 'z'
- confusing 'c' and 'k'
- confusing 'g' and 'j'.

If this happens, just keep prompting and doing activities that strengthen your child's knowledge – don't lose patience, eventually they will get it right.

Repetition

In certain circumstances, rote learning, or constant repetition of letters, may be the only answer to help a child who has extreme difficulty in remembering sounds. In cases like this, tradition has its benefits and a chant or song associated with the alphabet letters can be useful.

Should reading and writing be taught together?

Reading is fundamental to an appreciation of language but it cannot be taught in isolation. Reading and writing go hand in hand; as abilities in one develop, so too should abilities in the other.

- If one skill is developed at the expense of the other, you run the risk of reducing ability and understanding of language as a whole.

Remember, then, as you do activities with your child include some that will also develop writing skills. For example, when you teach a letter or a word allow your child to practise its formation on paper. The knowledge gained will not only be good writing practice but will also feed back into reading.

Strengthening skills

As your child gains ability in reading stories it is likely that he will want to write his own. At this point, the basic attempts he makes will be enhanced by activities that strengthen writing ability. So, don't forget to give some attention to:

- simple spellings
- sentence structure

- capital letters
- full stops.

If any of these areas becomes a problem for you, simply do the best you can, as every little bit of knowledge is helpful to your child. Taken together, all this will help to develop verbal expression, literacy and a sophisticated appreciation of language.

DRAWING AND VISUAL AIDS

If you ask an adult to draw a picture, unless they have some previous experience or aptitude for drawing, they will most likely feel that their attempts are not very good. Ask a child to draw a picture and they will do it happily without any fear of embarrassment. As far as they are concerned, whatever the drawing might be of, it's a good drawing and one to be proud of.

Remember:

- Children have a natural inclination to draw as a means of expression.

Occasionally, the inclination to draw develops into artistic ability but for the majority of individuals it wanes as the years pass.

What this means is that drawing is extremely important in the educational development of your child. It isn't a 'soft option' for an activity when you can't think of anything else to do – on the contrary, it is essential.

How to use drawing
Drawing activities, which will extend over several sessions, could include:

- Making a little book with a letter of the alphabet on each page and with each of the letters heavily illustrated and coloured. Keep in mind what was said about the teaching of the alphabet previously. Don't try and complete the book too quickly and do the activity in conjunction with plenty of stories that provide real examples of the letters.

Pointing at words while reading

Children tend to lose concentration easily. Their minds wander to something totally irrelevant like what they did yesterday or they can get sidetracked by the illustrations next to the text. They can also be attracted by the words surrounding the one they are actually reading. This is all unavoidable and, in fact, quite normal. Pointing helps to keep a child's concentration focused for longer periods of time. Make sure, therefore, that your child is using some form of pointing as it will enhance his perception of the text.

Line guides

This is one of the simplest teaching aids that you can make. Take a piece of card approximately two and a half centimetres by 15 centimetres. Use white card and then let your child colour it in. It is particularly useful for those children whose attention wanders to a different line as they are reading. A line guide is also useful when a child can't keep his finger moving steadily along a line.

Alice uses a line guide

Alice sat alongside six-year-old Ben as they read a story together. 'As we read, Ben, you point at the words, okay?'

'Okay,' said Ben, who was able to read quite a lot of the words on the page himself.

Carrying on with the story, Ben's finger moved slowly along the line as he and Alice took turns to read but then two lines lower his finger appeared to go down towards the corner of the page.

Alice tried again, several times, but the same thing happened.

Fig. 7. Line guide.

After talking to Ben's teacher, Alice made a line guide with Ben, coloured in and with the name 'Ben' written thickly on the front. The next story session, Alice tried using the line guide. To her surprise, it worked very well and Ben was able to scan more easily along the line, only moving down to the next line in the story at the right times.

Safety first

If a child is using any implement to make something, consider whether he is in fact old enough to understand any danger involved. If necessary, show him how to use the implement **safely** by holding it away from his body and not waving it about — given the opportunity, some children will walk around a room while unthinkingly waving a sharp pencil. Where appropriate, use implements or substances that are designed for children — from about six years of age onwards a child can begin to use glue sticks and blunt-nosed scissors.

Until your child is able to understand what he is doing, supervise him and don't leave him alone for even a few moments — it only takes a few seconds for a child to get entangled in sticky tape or worse! When in doubt, you do the difficult parts that require a degree of manual dexterity, such as cutting or joining. After finishing an activity clear away, out of your child's reach, any implements or substances that have been used.

Using flashcards

These are particularly good for very young children when you are just starting out with reading activities. A pack of cards might consist of a variety of pictures. If you have a camera, or you are good at drawing, then it is not difficult to make some interesting versions of your own. These could consist of pictures of places, family or animals.

For pre-beginners

- *Game 1:* Ask your child to name the object shown.

For beginners

- *Game 2:* If the picture is of a ball ask them to match it with a 'b' in a second pile of cards.

- *Game 3:* Have a second pile of cards with the whole name of the object or place written, the aim being to match the name to its picture. This helps children to identify words as a whole — make sure your child knows the constituent sounds as well.

Letter cards

A simple idea using letter cards is to prepare 24 pieces of blank paper in advance and then let your child copy the small alphabet letters onto them, perhaps using different pencil colours for different letters.

Similar sounds

One of the best ways to use flashcards to improve reading is to concentrate on words that have the same, or similar, sounds − with each word written on a different card. So you could introduce words that have an 'oo' sound in them, such as: 'boot', 'hoot', and 'foot'. The slight variation in pronunciation in words like 'foot' can be explained, if your child asks, by replying that sometimes we say the word slightly differently but it's still the same sound made with an 'oo'. After a few presentations, the words will be remembered and you can introduce another sound such as 'ee'. The words can later be mixed together for other word activities.

Expanding the activity

After finishing a letter game, Mrs Abdul asked Hasina if she could think of any other words that have an 'oo' sound in them. At first she didn't get the correct answer, so she prompted a little by pointing to a book and saying: 'What is this? Does this have an 'oo' sound?' The next session she tried, Hasina gave the correct answer. So Mrs Abdul used other items from around the house with an 'oo' sound in them. After that, feeling pleased with the progress her daughter was making, Mrs Abdul had a go with an 'ee' sound, collecting other real objects to surprise and educate in a similar way − a shoe heel, a seed and a weed from the garden.

Putting it together

The points covered in this chapter, so far, are all linked and will have an effect on one another as illustrated in Figure 8.

Fig. 8. How learning activities are linked

STRUCTURING YOUR APPROACH

There is a definite order in which your child needs to acquire the various reading skills. The games suggested in the next section reflect this approach.

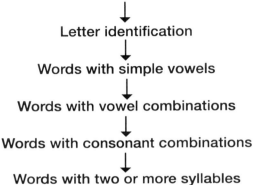

↓
Letter identification
↓
Words with simple vowels
↓
Words with vowel combinations
↓
Words with consonant combinations
↓
Words with two or more syllables

In case this seems a bit obscure, a vowel is one of the letters:

a e i o u

And a consonant is any letter that is not a vowel:

b c d f g . . .

A syllable is another way of saying how many sounds a word has – so the word 'but' has one sound or syllable, while the word 'butter' has two sounds or syllables (butt . . .er). Teach 'but' before you teach 'butter'.

- To make the point clear to your child that one word can have more than one sound, clap your hands for each sound. So for 'butter' you'd clap twice.

Keeping it simple

The level of difficulty of the games you choose will depend on the ability of your child but, when in doubt, keep it simple. There are many two and three letter words which children need to know first in order to gain a rudimentary skill in reading and sometimes it is necessary to go back to them to strengthen understanding.

Words with vowels, vowel combinations and consonant combinations are given at the end of the book (see **Simple Vocabulary**).

LEARNING LETTERS WITH SIMPLE IDEAS AND GAMES

1. Rings

Make ten small rings of paper joined with sticky tape. Write a lower-case letter on each ring in a simple bold print. Place a ring on each of your fingers. Have some objects, or pictures of objects ready, laid out in front of you and your child. Let your child say what the object is and then let her choose the ring you are wearing that corresponds with the letter the object name begins with.

2. Fishing

Take some letter cards and attach a paper clip to each. Place these in a bowl. Fix a small magnet to the end of a piece of string which in turn is attached to a small length of wood. Your child is now ready to go fishing for letters. As he picks a letter, he has to think of something that starts with that letter. If he gets it right, he can keep the letter. If he gets it wrong, it has to be put back in the bowl.

3. Finishing the word

Using letter cards, after your child knows a sound such as 'oo', form the first part of the word *eg poo_, coo_, too_*. Placing a 'l' card at the end successfully completes the word. If your child can do this then use words with different endings *eg soo_, boo_, hoo_*. Obviously, there are several possibilities for the last letter but always go for the simplest to begin with – which could give you: *soon, boot, hoot.* Following this, you can present other possible endings, such as: *soot, book, hoop.*

You can also miss out the beginning of the word in a similar manner and you can miss out the middle of the word, where a vowel or vowel combination is required *eg h_t (hit, hot, hat, hut),* or *b_ _t (boat, beat).*

The next stage is beginning words with consonant combinations, such as 'ch' and 'st'. Only move onto games with these sounds when your child has grasped the idea about how to use basic vowel sounds with single consonants.

4. Joining the letter

Write down a series of letters and ask your child to join up, with a line, any letters that are the same.

To get your child used to the idea, shapes or pictures can also be used. See Figure 9.

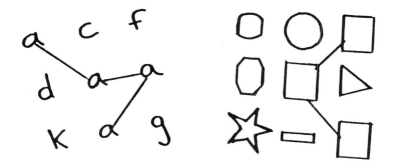

Fig. 9. Joining letters and shapes.

5. What's the same?

Collect some small, safe objects from around the house that begin with the same letter such as sunglasses, salt-shaker, sausage (cold!), sandwich, stamp, spoon. Ask your child, when he tells you what they are, whether he can also tell you something that's the same about the words he is saying − prompt if necessary. Then draw the letter on a large sheet of paper. Let your child copy the letter. He can also put little versions of the letter around the large letter as a form of illustration.

Alternatively, either your version or his version − or both − can be coloured in. To make it slightly easier, when you draw the letter use double lines then your child can colour between the lines.

A more sophisticated version of this is to use small bits of coloured tissue paper or glitter to fill in the letter − but keep in mind the safety aspect and make sure that you supervise throughout.

6. Is it there?

Collect several objects, or pictures of objects, from around the house. These might be: a book, a watch, an orange, a radio, a pot (or potty), a spoon, a sweet. Then have the first letter of the name of each object written on a large sheet of paper, in double lines, along with some other letters.

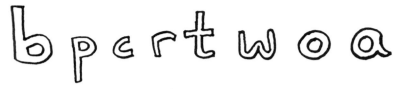

Fig. 10. Double letters.

Ask your child to colour in the letter if there is an object that begins with that particular letter.

7. Tracks

Draw two parallel lines with divisions that look similar to railway tracks. The lines can be drawn in any direction (in straight lines, as below, or with curves). Put a different letter in some of the squares formed, whilst leaving others blank.

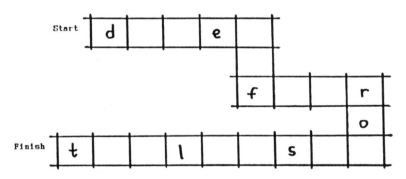

Fig. 11. Game of tracks.

Using a counter each, throw dice to take turns to move along the track. When a player lands on a square with a letter, they have to say a word that begins with that letter. Alternatively, word cards can be used. The first player to get to the end of the track is the winner.

The difficulty of the game can be altered by using more or fewer squares and letters. Letters can also appear more than once.

Another version of the game is to give a word for the letter landed on and spell it out. This can be done either verbally or with letter cards.

You can make the game more interesting by having penalties, such as moving one position back for a wrong answer.

Though throwing a game has a certain unethical quality, generally speaking, if you keep on winning your child will lose his motivation quite quickly – and the aim is to help reading skills, not for you to win the game! Therefore, engineer it so that sometimes your child wins a proportion of the games as well as you.

8. Picture sort

Take several medium-sized envelopes and mark the front with a lower-case letter. Then, using old magazine or catalogue pictures, that you have carefully cut out, ask your child what sound the item in the picture begins with. He then places a correct letter card in the appropriate envelope. So, if the picture is of a ball, a 'b' letter card goes in the envelope with a 'b' on the front.

9. Find the letter

Have a bag of letter cards beside you and your child as you are sharing a story together. Choose a letter from a word you are reading, saying the small letter sound clearly and distinctly. Ask your child to find the letter in the bag of letter cards. Give plenty of praise – showing the correct letter if necessary – then carry on with the story.

10. Tracing

Take some tracing or greaseproof paper and place a rectangle of it over a page of a children's book. Fix this in place with paper clips. You can also form a page with letters on it yourself. Using a good pencil, let your child trace over the letters.

CASE STUDIES

Mary thinks about words

Over the last few weeks, Mary had really enjoyed reading with Sophie, and they'd even started making up stories together. But, whenever Sophie read a few lines on her own, Mary noticed that her daughter had trouble with certain words – even though sometimes she could say the first part of the word.

One quiet evening, after putting Sophie to bed, Mary looked at a story-book more closely. She discovered that the problem words usually had more than one syllable – words like *butter, throwing* and *carpet*. Sophie knew some of these types of words, and she was obviously getting knowledge from school, but she needed more practice. Mary decided that over the weekend she would use some letter cards to show Sophie how little words

− like car and pet − could be made into big words − like carpet. And how adding an 'ing' ending is useful in many words.

How Sam learnt some letters with flashcards

There were two picture cards in front of Sam.

'What is this picture of?' said Tracy, pointing to the first card.

'A dog, Mummy,' Sam answered happily.

Tracy pointed to the second card. 'And what is this picture of?'

'It's a big horse with a lot of hair.'

'That's right Sam. Now, when you said the word *dog*, what sound did you say first?'

Sam looked puzzled as he thought very hard.

After a few moments without a reply, Tracy said, 'Does it begin with a "suh", like "Suh" for "Sam"?'

'No,' Sam answered.

'Does it begin with a "kuh"?'

'No.'

'What about "guh"?'

Sam screwed his face up in concentration and then replied, 'No.'

'Do you think it begins with a "duh" − think hard before you say?'

'Yes, that's it, Mummy. It's "duh" − "duh" for *doggy*. I got it right, didn't I?'

'You sure did,' said Tracy, smiling.

Bill and Kevin draw a picture

'So, Kevin? What do you think about that nasty Mr Ruggles and what he did to the animals?'

Kevin's eyebrows moved up and down as he considered his answer. 'Well . . . he wasn't very nice.'

'No, he wasn't very nice at all,' said Bill. 'But, can you tell me why you think he wasn't very nice?'

Kevin thought hard. 'Well . . . he was nasty to the animals and . . . Jim also, who was looking after them, and . . .'

Bill looked on expectantly.

'Um,' said Kevin, then fell silent.

'That's all true,' replied Bill, feeling a bit put out that Kevin didn't seem to have understood the story. 'Can you think of anything else about him?'

Kevin shook his head and frowned.

'Tell you what, let's draw a picture of the story and put into it all the things that you can think of that are important.'

Reaching for some paper and coloured pencils, Kevin said, 'Okay, Dad.'

To Bill's amazement, within a few minutes, Kevin had produced a really good picture that showed all the main characters of the story and depicted the things that they had done. Kevin had understood more than Bill first thought – he just didn't have the language to express himself.

POINTS FOR DISCUSSION

1. Letters are like building blocks. So it's important to learn the sounds of letters before the names of letters, and lower-case letters before upper-case letters. But can children also learn simple, whole words at the same time?

2. Why do you think it's important for children to practise writing letters as well as reading them?

3. There are many materials that can be used to help in teaching letters and reading, such as flashcards, letter cards, wall friezes and line guides. What do you think it is that makes them so useful?

4
Using Books, Toys and Games

MATCHING BOOKS TO YOUR CHILD'S ABILITY

How many times have you gone into a bookseller and been confused by
the sheer volume of children's books that are available to choose from?
And, even if you have chosen something that you think is correct, did
your child read it or did he place it in a cupboard – behind the unopened
box of hankies he received as a birthday present from a distant aunt?

Choosing books at the appropriate level for your child is not difficult,
it just takes a bit of thought – *how* you choose is just as important as *what*
you choose.

What interests your child?

Think about the things your child likes about stories and books. These
might be:

- colourful pages
- simple illustrations
- heavily drawn illustrations
- to laugh at a funny story
- action and a fast pace
- a slow pace
- stories about people
- stories about events
- stories about other children
- stories centering around mysterious happenings
- stories about castles, schools or strange buildings
- interesting places or countries
- stories with animal characters
- stories with adult characters
- factual books about machines or the world around us.

Introducing variety

If your child asks for certain types of books, it is important to follow up his interest with occasional trips to the local bookshop or library. Never be afraid, though, to try and influence his reading by suggesting other classes of books or titles that you feel would be beneficial. Aim for an all-round exposure to a variety of books and stories. There is plenty of time, later, for your child to develop a specific liking for a particular type of story, which might, for example, be based on comedy or science fiction.

The right level

For the child just beginning to read, it is important to consider not only the interests she has – which will inform your choice – but also the text of the book. Is it going to be too easy or too hard to read?

- A child should be able to cope with about 60 per cent of the words without too much prompting.

This is a loose estimate and obviously you can help with many of the difficult words, but if she is struggling with virtually all the words then it is too hard for her and you should choose another, easier, book.

Tricky words

One of the points at which many parents fail when choosing books is that they assume that all small words are easy to read. They tend to forget how tricky certain words can be and that some letter combinations will make different sounds in different words:

For example:

- *Who* is sounded like *hoo* and not *woo*.

- *One* and *won* are sounded like *wun*.

- *Why* is sounded like *Y*.

Looking closely

When you are choosing a book try and think like a child and consider whether it is, in fact, a book with enough easy words.

Look at the number of syllables the words have. As previously mentioned, there is a definite order to the acquisition of various reading skills (see page 58). Therefore, children need to learn a variety of one syllable words before they can move on to two syllable words. If you find a book that has a mixture of one and two or more syllable words, consider its use very carefully. It is quite common, these days, to find heavily illustrated books that have single and multi-syllable words in a very slim text, with only a few words on each page. For example:

The dog finished his bone as the elephant went by.

The text appears to be for a beginner reader but young children often can't cope with this type of presentation. Even if they manage to memorise the words, with the help of the pictures, they are unable to transfer the necessary logic to other words in other books. These books are sometimes based on the real books approach and are looked at in greater detail further on.

Some difficult words are good
An important exception to avoiding difficult words in the text is when a word is used *repeatedly* throughout the book. It may be a word on which the storyline rests or it may be a character name. The repetition allows your child to become familiar with the word.

Firing imagination
When you are choosing a children's book that you will be reading, go for something that will interest and excite − and whet your child's appetite for more.

Fact or fiction books?

Reading is only a part of education and there is a multitude of books written for children on every conceivable subject. Their use should never be overlooked in favour of stories alone. These books could be about:

- the weather
- sound and hearing
- dinosaurs and archaeology
- space
- cars
- buildings
- baby animals
- machines
- places.

The books are pitched at different ages and will often have this noted somewhere on the cover. Use this as a guide and then consider the text in the same way as discussed above. It almost goes without saying that there would be little point in using a book that has solid blocks of text when your child is still having trouble with some of his letters.

Reading interesting facts together

Besides your child reading an information book on his own, you can read and look at the pictures together as you would an ordinary story. Remember, though, that a young child's tolerance for learning facts may not be the same as that for reading or listening to a story, so you may have to shorten the activity length.

Poems and rhymes – they're also written in lines!

Most parents will use a nursery rhyme with their young child at some stage. It is a sad fact, though, that as a child matures the use of poems and rhymes becomes less popular. It may be that some parents don't have particularly good memories of poetry at school and this colours their thinking. But, there is a wealth of enjoyable material available nowadays that has been specially written for children of all ages and their use should always be considered when choosing material.

Rhymes develop reading
Poems and rhymes are useful because they:

- Provide verbal stimulation to the developing mind.

- Have a simple rhyming structure which is easily picked up.

- Often use bright and bold illustrations that are fun.

- Provide a pleasant surprise, as reading speed increases, when children realise that the words they are reading actually rhyme.

Looking at pictures

Consider whether the illustrations are fairly simple and straightforward or whether they're too complex for your child. When in doubt, go for simplicity.

The same is true for 'how to' books, where the instructions for making something – for example, by folding paper – should be simple enough for your child to understand even if she needs some help in the construction.

Carmen looks at the pictures

With a book open in each hand, Carmen was having trouble deciding which book to buy for five-year-old Julie. This is no good, she thought, I'll be here all day unless I choose. Then Carmen decided to do it logically and considered: Would Julie like these books? Yes, no doubt about that. They're both excellent stories. Would she like the way the characters are drawn? Carmen looked at the book in her left hand. Um, this one's a bit densely drawn with lots of line markings. Julie likes less fiddly pictures. I think I'll take this other one.

Is it really interesting?

When trying to assess how interesting a children's book is, consider that:

- 'The cat sat on the mat' is quite interesting

but, to a child:

- 'The *fat* cat sat on his *hat*' is much more interesting because it's more descriptive and it's funnier. It is also a sentence with simple words that are easy to understand. If there is a good picture as well, then the text is enhanced.

Be critical

The ability to use very basic language but tell a good story is down to the skill of the author; there are good children's authors and there are bad ones – so always choose carefully.

When choosing a book, remember to check:

(a) the use of easy and hard words
(b) the use of single and multi-syllable words
(c) how interesting the story is
(d) how colourful and descriptive the pictures are.

Keep the pace up
Simple readers should not be used exclusively and you should occasionally be reading stories of greater sophistication to your child, above his level of ability. If you sometimes use an active method (see page 42) then the whole learning process is speeded up.

Traditional or modern stories?

This has been a controversial area in recent years with many of our favourite characters, such as Winnie The Pooh and Peter Pan, criticised as being twee and old fashioned. It is true that many traditional stories and fairy tales may not reflect the multi-class and multi-ethnic values that we now know to be important. However, many of these stories are about individuals and their personal characteristics and, simply put, whether they're good or bad. The story's ability to look at individuals in this way, while being entertaining, is what has given many of them their universal appeal and classic status.

Good stories always return
Schools are now beginning to use more traditional stories, alongside modern stories, as there is a growing realisation that exposure to a wide variety of literature is beneficial to the developing child.

So if you enjoyed a particular story when you were younger and would like to use it with your child, don't be put off by fashion. Traditional stories in the form of legends, fairy tales and more recent classics, keep returning precisely because they were enjoyed by previous generations and they therefore have something to offer the next generation too.

Reading at school

Schools encourage children to read a variety of material to gain reading experience. But to teach reading they will often use a reading scheme – a series of books graded in difficulty. Children often bring these home for homework.

Because of the cost involved in buying a reading scheme, though, many of them are now dated. And it can be several years or more before a school replaces them. So, what you choose and use provides good backup to school work.

Building on schoolwork

When choosing books from the shops or the library keep in mind what your child is doing in school but don't feel you have to copy it. The support and motivation that you provide is as important as your choice of books. And remember, if you learnt to read and enjoy books in a certain way, then your child is also likely to benefit from a similar approach.

USING COMICS AND COMPUTERS

Comics and computer games have received a bad press. This is unfortunate. There is nothing intrinsically wrong with these or any other childhood interest.

Comics are useful because they can:

A. Enhance language appreciation − *if there is a moderate amount of text.*

B. Develop children's imagination and interests − *helped by the highly graphic and stylised images.*

● Do you remember, as a child, spending a lazy afternoon with a bar of chocolate, some sweets and the latest comic? Don't let your child miss out − it's good fun and it develops reading skills too.

Computer games are useful because they can:

A. Increase mental agility − *thinking faster.*

B. Develop hand-eye coordination − *that is, children learn to move quicker in response to something they see.*

Computers and language

Computers are not just about playing games and a good system can be used to learn more about language use or even to write, edit and print a child's own story. This is often an activity in the school classroom and can be highly enjoyable.

Keeping a balance

Having said that comics and computers are good, it is still a question of finding a balance. When children begin to use these activities to the exclusion of other normal childhood activities, then that is the time when problems can occur. Children need to be stimulated with a variety of different things in order to promote healthy mental development.

Dayna withdraws!

'I really don't know what to do,' said Lee, to Dayna's teacher, Mrs Shah. 'She seems to rarely say anything at all lately and when she does it doesn't invite any sort of extended answer.'

Mrs Shah looked thoughtful. 'I've noticed it too, in class. Can you think of any reason why Dayna might have started behaving like this? Can you date it to any event that happened?'

'No, not really. Home life ticks along as normal without any major upheavals. In fact, I'm doing well at work and got a rise some months back. I've even had more cash to spend on the family and bought Dayna a computer. It's got all the latest games and gadgets like Internet. She loves it and I know it's doing her maths a power of good – I spoke to Mr Davies only last week and he's very pleased with her progress.'

'How much time does Dayna spend using the computer?'

'Oh, I'm not sure exactly but she's a good girl and always puts in a lot of work – she wants to make something of herself does Dayna.'

'Does she play sports at all, go out with friends?'

'Not as much as she used to.'

Mrs Shah considered what she had just been told about Dayna, then said, as tactfully as possible, 'You know, it could be that we need to provide some more variety in what Dayna does. She's getting good experience on the computer but a little balance to develop her imagination and ideas may help her to be more communicative again. Do you think you could help Dayna with that?'

'To play some sports and get more friends over? I think I could help with that. If you think it will help?'

'Oh I do. I most certainly do!'

Making your child aware

Activities don't just teach a child how to do something – they also teach her how to respond to other people – parents, friends, teachers – who may also be engaged in a part of the task. The social awareness a child gains through education is just as important as any reading and practical skills she may learn from books, toys and computer games.

Does your child have a balanced day?

Place a tick by each of the activities your child is regularly engaged in. Then work out the amount of time spent on the activity. It's likely that your child won't have exactly the same timetable every day – in which case, you can look at two or three days together to find his 'ideal' day.

Activity	✓orX	Time
Sleeping – eight hours minimum	_____	_____
Eating – three good meals	_____	_____
Exercise – not necessarily every day but regular and not to total exhaustion	_____	_____
Watching TV – a moderate amount to inform and entertain	_____	_____
Using a computer – to develop abilities and entertain	_____	_____
Being with family and friends – to develop communication and social skills	_____	_____
School – for knowledge, social and communication skills and future work prospects	_____	_____
Reading – in and out of school, to inform and entertain	_____	_____
Hobbies and pastimes – to develop wider interests		
Other	_____	_____

SELECTING AND USING TOYS AND OTHER MATERIALS

The more motivated a child is by what she is doing the more she is likely to learn. You can enhance motivation by using toys, objects or pictures that enliven your activities.

Linking reading and toys

When choosing items, think about:

- How they relate to what you want to achieve. Try and create some sort of a link.

Examples

1. If you are telling a story about a little girl and her adventures, you could use a doll or soft toy to emphasise the role of the characters.

2. If you are teaching letters then some three dimensional plastic or wooden alphabet letters can be beneficial. These can be used in the same way as letter cards.

With pictures and flashcards, either bought or produced yourself, make sure that they are about something that is of interest to your child. Young children are often interested in animals and these can be a good starting point for an activity.

Buying useful items

Whether you are buying a book, a toy, or a game, consider the following questions:

(a) Does it have a strong construction or is it well made?

(b) Does it do what it's supposed to do?

(c) Does it teach something and/or entertain?

(d) Is safe to use, without such things as colours rubbing off?

(e) Is it uncomplicated and can it be used easily by your child?

(f) Is it likely to have a long life, with your child using it again and again?

(g) Does it fit into your education aims for your child's future, in some way?

Choosing materials

The most versatile material is plain paper. Use it for:

- drawing
- writing
- folding
- crumpling – if you're feeling a bit artistic.

5
Supporting Your Child's Reading

GETTING CHILDREN'S INTEREST

To get your child's interest you need to be a source of motivation. This doesn't mean you have to be an all round entertainer but it does mean that you have to be aware of your child's reactions to what you are doing.

If you are observant then you can make your approach:

- flexible
- inspiring.

The idea is to make your child think: **I want to know more about that.**

Keeping attention

Young children often have a short attention span. You can do a great deal, though, simply by being aware of when your child is becoming bored. At this point either stop or change to a different activity. This will allow your child to approach the next activity fresh and eager to participate.

Developing and extending interest

There are a number of ways to do this:

- Find a topic that your child enjoys and work activities around it.

- Locate the areas of weakness in reading and pay particular attention to these to build up confidence.

- Make the activity fun – whether it is formal or informal – and demonstrate that you are enjoying it as well.

- Use humour – most children like to laugh at funny stories and games.

Kelsy has a long face

A frown crossed Kelsy's face and a fixed, sullen expression replaced her normal smile. Heather felt annoyed. After all, she'd spoken to Mr Gregson, Kelsy's teacher, and knew exactly what the problem was. She just didn't know how to get the information about the 'o' sound across to Kelsy without having a very unhappy little girl on her hands. Heather sighed, decided enough was enough for one day, and went to the kitchen to make herself a cup of coffee. A few minutes later she was sipping her drink with her feet up and reading the paper. Then Heather burst out laughing.

Kelsy came rushing in. 'What are you laughing about, Mummy?'

'Oh, nothing much. Just something funny in the paper.'

'What? What?' pleaded Kelsy, 'tell me?'

'Well . . .', Heather paused for a moment and realised that for the first time she had Kelsy's undivided attention. She laughed again, 'It's about potatoes.'

'Potatoes!' Kelsy repeated, now also laughing along with her mother.

'Yes. See? It says in big letters right there. Let's look at it together.' And as Heather pointed they read the headline: OH NO NOT MORE POTATOES!

With a little bit more fun attention, the 'o' problem was soon fixed.

Don't rush it

If your child asks a question, respond, and give him time to think about what you have said and come back to you for any clarification.

Don't feel under any pressure to get to the next stage of an activity. It could well be that your child is coming to grips with something of importance and needs time to work it out. Obviously, there are times when you will want to get across important information without distraction but don't let this override the positive development of a questioning mind.

- Above all, always give encouragement and praise – whether your child has completed the task perfectly or not.

LEARNING IN AND OUT OF SCHOOL

Having read a fair part of this book, you are probably wondering whether much of what has been suggested is not the responsibility of the school? Well, to a large extent, it is but bear in mind that:

1. The ultimate responsibility for your child's education rests with you.

2. There are good schools and good teachers and there are bad schools and bad teachers – not necessarily in the same place.

3. Perhaps most importantly, the vast majority of good teachers work under a significant amount of pressure.

Reading and the National Curriculum

In UK state schools, primary school teachers are required to teach according to the National Curriculum, which in essence is a syllabus and assessment procedure for different age groups. These are sometimes referred to as Key Stages (KS). Primary schools cover KS1 and KS2.

	KS1 (5–7 years)	KS2 (7–11 years)
English	levels 1–3	levels 2–5

A big change

Although there are problems with implementation, the structured approach the National Curriculum offers is welcomed by many teachers. But it is going to take some time to iron out all the bugs as well as get the balance right between time spent teaching and time spent assessing.

Unfortunately many schools do not have the funds to do all the activities they would like with the appropriate books or materials. In addition to this, some schools have an average of 30 children in a class and there is simply not the time to give each child all the individual attention required. Teachers do a great job though, having planned the class curriculum and adapted parts of it according to individual needs. They are sometimes helped in this by part-time support and volunteer parents.

Reading and other skills

Reading represents only one part of the National Curriculum in English, which is separated into five areas, known as **Statements of Attainment.**

These are:

1. speaking and listening
2. reading
3. writing
4. spelling
5. handwriting.

Each of these areas is split into levels. Your child will pass from one level to the next as he becomes more competent.

Language and reading skills are connected

Keep in mind that, though the divisions in the National Curriculum exist in order to make teaching and learning easier, many of the skills learnt in one area will have a knock-on effect in others. For example, strengthening your child's skill in listening to a story or an instruction will help to develop understanding of storylines and how characters interact.

Reading practice in school

If a child gets ten minutes a week to read with the class teacher and there are 30 children in a class, this means that the class teacher has to set aside five hours a week for reading – a whole day (remember: lunch and playtime also take up part of the day). For many teachers this is an impossibility. It goes without saying, too, that ten minutes reading a week is not enough to develop language and reading skills. If you consider as well that two or three children in a class may require remedial help then it can be seen how the problem is easily compounded for many children.

How is reading taught in school?
In reality, many children get more than ten minutes a week reading as the majority of good teachers will find some way to work reading into other subjects as well as having whole class activities with reading as a subsidiary activity. Reading practice will also be gained from a well organised reading system. To a large extent this is all down to the management skill of the teacher. So, when you look at what your child is doing in school, remember:

- There can be wide variation in attainment between schools based on teaching quality.

- Different schools will value reading activities differently – some schools will stress the importance of silent reading sessions; others the importance of combined reading sessions, with several years participating; while other schools will do nothing.

Get a buddy
'What a great idea Mrs Sharpe, the new headmistress, has for combined reading sessions,' said Sunita to Nicola as they waited for their children outside the school gate. 'The older children help the younger ones with their reading as a "buddy". And, she says, it promotes a sense of accomplishment and importance in the older children as well as allowing the younger children to relate to someone who is closer to them in age and experience. My two really enjoy reading since the system was introduced.'

Nicola nodded in agreement. 'Yes, it does seem to be a very good idea and many of the teachers say it also helps to create a greater sense of harmony in the school. Makes you wonder why it wasn't done before?'

The nuts and bolts of reading
Besides developing skills through experience, time must be spent learning the mechanics of reading. To this end, there are three main approaches that schools use. These are:

1. phonics
2. look and say
3. real books.

Phonics

The **phonics** method has a long tradition stretching back many years and stresses the sounding and identification of letters and letter groups, like 'l', 'ea' and 'ch'. It is widely accepted as being the better method for the majority of children. Reading schemes used in schools are often based on the Phonics method.

However, it does have limitations. For example, children have limited scope to develop their own understanding of language – at least initially – and complex words don't always conform to phonic rules. Compare the pronounciation of the words:

rough   cough   bough   fought

Look and say

The **look and say** method uses whole word recognition activities (flashcard games) – based on the idea that children will learn to recognise some words as a whole.

Real books

The **real books** method uses ordinary picture books – with children encouraged to choose their own – to stimulate enjoyment of stories and the identification of letters and words through the sharing of books with an adult.

Schools today

The importance of the **look and say** and **real books** methods as the prime methods of teaching reading skills is now declining, although not everywhere. They became very popular during the late 1960s and early 1970s when a variety of new methods was experimented with. The main problem with them, as suggested earlier in this book, is that children rely very heavily on the pictures and what they learn is not easily transferable to other texts. Left to their own devices, it is unlikely that children will suddenly become competent readers. They need instruction.

Having said that, look and say activities are useful when some difficult words are proving hard to learn. Similarly, real books can be useful as they are often colourful and provide the child with an interesting story – but they need to be used wisely.

What works best?

The best method of teaching reading, which many schools are now using, is to have the phonics method as the prime method of teaching with the use of other learning styles to add variety. In other words, a mixture of approaches. This book is based on this idea. So, if you are using letter cards to produce a word, such as 'let', and sounding each letter with its lower-case sound, then you are using the **phonics** method. If you are using flashcards with a whole word displayed, such as 'boat' (whole word recognition activities), then you are using a **look and say** method. As long as you stick to *mainly* using the phonics method, reading skills will develop.

Helping the teacher

Even if you don't want to devote a great deal of time to teaching reading skills directly, there are still things you can do to ensure that your child's progress continues:

- Make sure that reading homework is done.

- Fill out any record cards that your child brings home.

- Help with making word cards, sent home in an envelope or box, into interesting or funny sentences.

- Make sure that your child is enjoying reading. If not, find out why.

- See the teacher occasionally. Make sure she knows about your child's interests and how they are developing.

- Don't get exasperated if your child brings the same book home several times, it's practice and the teacher is encouraging it.

- Don't get annoyed with the teacher because another parent may have told you about their child being on a harder book in a reading scheme than your child is. As long as progress is being made, that's good enough.

- If you have the time and want to become more involved, become a volunteer class helper.

Learning out of school

The ability to read and use language well has a great deal to do with an individual's knowledge of the world around her. So, any time that you spend with your child outside planned or formal activities, away from home or school, can have positive educational benefits:

- Do different things together – walking the dog or doing some local sightseeing. This will prompt questions that help a child to think more deeply about the activity she is engaged in.

- Have some sort of answer for your questioning child – if you don't know the answer, say you don't know and find out for the future – you may even discover some new interesting facts yourself!

Keep communicating

Whenever possible, talk to your child. Real communication – with different locations as a stimulus – is vitally important as a promoter of language, reading and general educational ability.

Thinking round an activity

Give thought to how the activity can link more specifically into your aims, then play a game accordingly.

Examples

A. Before you go shopping at the supermarket, ask your child to draw pictures of the things you need. Help him to write some of the names of the items.

B. On a journey, ask your child to look at all the street signs that you pass and see if she can find one that begins with a certain letter or says a certain word like **'stop'** or **'go'**.

C. Play a game of I-Spy: I-Spy with my little eye something beginning with the letter . . . , can you guess what it is?

Remember
- Every moment that you spend together is valuable and has the potential to increase basic skills and awareness.

Do's and don'ts of reading support

Listed below are a few **do's** and **don'ts** that you should keep in mind as you help or oversee your child's reading:

Do
- Make sure that your child's reading is progressing at a reasonable rate.

- Talk to the school when you have a concern.

- Motivate and stimulate your child's interest with fun activities and a variety of stories and books.

- Teach a reading skill when you believe it's necessary.

- Remember that children learn formally and informally and that going to different places can promote learning.

- Involve your child with activities or reading that you are engaged in.

- Do remember that children are individuals. They progress at different rates and what works for one child may not work for another.

Don't
- Lose patience when your child makes mistakes.

- Worry too much about educational theories of reading.

- Use books that are way too hard for your child's level of ability.

- Stop your child from asking a reasonable amount of questions.

- Think that your child will suddenly read well – it takes work.

- Forget to give encouragement and praise whether your child has completed a task correctly or not.

- Forget to tell a bedtime story.

MEETING DIFFERENT CHILDREN'S NEEDS

Boys behave differently from girls. Some children come from different cultures. There are differences in the way parents bring up their children. Some children are more intelligent than others. All these things and more will affect how a child learns to read.

If my child is bright does she still need my help?

Education is not just about reading and language but about developing the whole person, with all that that entails. As a parent of an intelligent child, you are in a unique position to help because:

- A bright child can have difficulty in particular areas of her learning.
- There may be gaps in her learning.
- You can show how one area of learning links to others.

Gifted children

Children who are exceptionally bright – sometimes brighter and more intelligent than their parents – are termed gifted.

A gifted child is a child who has superior ability, beyond what would normally be expected for his age, in a particular field of endeavour. In other words, a child's giftedness can be displayed in a variety of areas, whether it be science, language, sport, craft, performing arts or anything else. Gifted children might also be exceptionally creative or productive thinkers. The extent of the giftedness will determine how proficient a child is in one or more fields.

Many children are gifted

According to Her Majesty's Inspectors in *Education Observed* (HMI, 1992) about five per cent of children are gifted in some way. We are not talking here about children at the genius level, although they need guidance just as much as anyone else, but simply about children who have highly developed ability. At this level in the population one child in 20 – approximately one or two children in every classroom – is in this category. Considering that there is little provision in this country for special education for gifted children, any help that you can provide is beneficial.

Children who are gifted:

- often learn to read easily and at a younger age than their friends

- may have a keen sense of humour

- are often quick to appreciate nuances and hidden meanings.

Parents can help

Much can be done by a parent, by supplying answers, interesting activities or appropriate books. This will help to satisfy curiosity as well as the desire for greater mental stimulation and more detailed knowledge.

Variation between boys and girls

Below the age of about nine or ten, educational ability is similar. Any differences that are observable in reading attainment are likely to be due to temperament. Girls tend to be slightly more able to apply themselves to the learning process, although this may be the result of family and school influences.

Recently a trend has emerged that is thought to be causing some worrying differences in achievement between boys and girls. It appears that:

- Parents are spending less time reading to their sons than to their daughters.

- Less time is spent discussing what sons are learning at school.

- Daughters are more likely to be bought books than sons.

- Boys are more likely to be attempting homework with a nearby distraction such as having the TV on.

Remember
Make sure that you avoid these pitfalls and treat your son or daughter in ways that will give them the maximum opportunity to succeed in tomorrow's demanding world.

Keeping your child's options open

Whether your child is a boy or a girl, they need the opportunity to read, learn and participate in a wide variety of subjects – with as little extreme bias as possible towards any one type of subject too early.

Mummy vacuums, daddy mends the car!
The bias within books that has sometimes been viewed as the root of later gender stereotyping (the tendency to follow traditionally male or female roles) may be part of the cause of later professional choice but it is not the whole cause. People choose to do certain types of jobs for a variety of reasons that in fact may have little to do with the type of books read as a child.

Don't be a harsh censor
Children like stories that they can identify with. Sometimes this is displayed by boys going for action-orientated stories and girls going for fantasy-orientated stories. Children will find their own level with these things and provided the books or comics are not blatantly gory, and your child is not reading them to the exclusion of anything else, then allow a certain amount of latitude.

Dipak gets the comic

'No. I won't have it! I won't have Dipak reading this rubbish,' Mrs Patel stated flatly to her husband.

'But look dear, it's pretty mild and he's going to read it anyway, whatever you do. He can get a copy from his friends or anywhere else.'

'I don't care. I don't want him reading comics with soldiers and guns and fighting in them.' She held up the offending comic and waved it under Mr Patel's nose. 'This is going straight in the dustbin – and that's the last of it!'

Mr Patel looked at his wife, smiled and gently took her hand. 'You think so, huh? Come with me.'

They went up the stairs and quietly entered Dipak's room. Wedged under the pillow, by the sleeping boy's head, was another action comic, while on the floor were three more.

Teaching brothers and sisters of different ages together

The age difference means that there is often a difference in reading ability and achievement level. This means that different activities – or different versions of the same activity – need to be done in order to maximise the learning session for each child. It can be accomplished but it will depend on the temperament of your children – whether they are quiet or boisterous – and whether they can interact well with each other.

If you find that teaching your children together is not working then the obvious alternative is to teach them separately. It may take a little more time and effort on your part, but it may prove more beneficial in the long-run.

Teaching twins and triplets

It might be thought that because these children are exactly the same age, as well as at the same educational standard, learning sessions can proceed smoothly. But doing any activities with brothers and sisters, born at the same time, presents unique difficulties because:

- The relationship between the children is extremely strong, which can have an effect on how they react to the learning process itself. For example, they may have specific problems in an aspect of their reading but instead of being able to work it out with your help, they may compound the problem for each other.

- If one twin finds something funny this is transmitted to the other, like a rubber ball that can't be stopped. In some cases, if you try to intervene, it can be perceived as an attempt to affect the children's intense personal relationship, making it even harder to help with their reading in subsequent learning sessions.

Your knowledge of the personalities of your children will help to reduce the chance of problems occuring in the first place, as you will be aware of the signs of annoyance and irritation. Furthermore, some twins and triplets work perfectly well together. But if problems do occur then be prepared to conduct separate learning sessions with each child. An additional positive outcome of this could be the development of greater individuality because their learning is taking a slightly different pathway.

Cultural variation and reading
There are many positive aspects to having children of various cultures learning together in a class. For example, inter-racial harmony is improved. But reading development for all the children in the class may be slowed due to the needs of individual children – some may not be able to use the English language properly yet and others may have difficulty with common sayings and expressions.

Being aware
If your child is an English speaker, and in this situation, it is important to be aware of what is going on at school and help him at home as much as possible.

If you are of a different nationality and are bilingual, and your child is attending school in this country, speak English as much as possible at home. In this way, there is greater chance your child will:

(a) become proficient in English as well as his ethnic language

(b) more easily integrate socially

(c) progress quicker in reading

(d) develop academically that much faster

BECOMING A FLUENT READER

There can be a wide variation in the attainment of reading fluency depending on the school your child attends and the environment in which he lives. This results from the:

- Policies or ethos of the school – dictating what is expected to be learnt and when.
- Locality – inner city or outlying district.
- Social problems that may exist in the district.
- Extent to which reading is valued in your family.
- Books and resources available
- Way in which the school deals with remedial problems.

Supporting reading means:

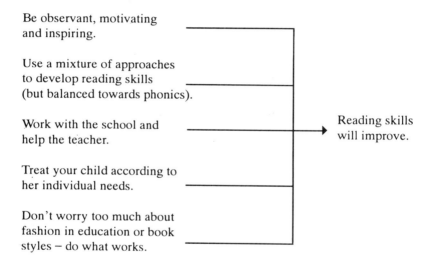

Be observant, motivating and inspiring.

Use a mixture of approaches to develop reading skills (but balanced towards phonics).

Work with the school and help the teacher.

Treat your child according to her individual needs.

Don't worry too much about fashion in education or book styles – do what works.

Reading skills will improve.

At what age should my child be able to read fluently?

In general, many primary schools aim to have children reading fluently by the age of eight or nine. In practice, schools often count themselves fortunate if they can achieve fluency in reading by the age of eleven – when most children will be changing to secondary schools. Good primary schools will be achieving a degree of fluency by the age of seven.

Certainly, if your child has not gained some grasp of the rudiments of reading by the age of seven, then you need to intervene and find out why.

Children are individuals
Keep in mind that any attempt to pigeonhole children into being able to carry out a particular reading task by a specific age is, by its nature, a generalisation. There can be considerable variation based not only on the above points, but also on level of maturity and special educational needs.

Reading age – what does it mean?
This is a formal method that is used to assess reading standard. So, a child can be said to have a reading age of, say, six. This means that a child would be expected to have the reading skills that most six-year-olds have, whatever his actual age is. Reading ages are useful when measuring improvement over time in conjunction with planned lessons or remedial help.
    They are:

- A statistical method where children are compared with group norms (figures based on what groups of children can do).

- A fair and more objective test than a straight teacher assessment.

- Unconnected to the attainment level of other children in the class.

But keep in mind that reading age tests:

- Cannot predict a child's ability to improve.

- Should not be used in isolation but form part of an overall educational assessment.

- Are not being used as an excuse for shoddy teaching – a child could be labelled as having a low reading age and sent for remedial help, when really all that he needs is a more understanding and capable teacher and a boost to his confidence.

ASSESSING READING PERFORMANCE

Besides making a comparison between your child's reading abilities and what you can remember doing as a child (see Chapter 1), you can also watch your child as he looks at books or words and consider whether he has the skills listed below. This list is not exhaustive so feel free to add new abilities as your child learns them. Remember, though, that this is not a test which is either passed or failed but simply a means of judging the level of attainment reached. Place a tick by the abilities when you're sure your child has gained them:

Pre-beginner ✓

- Can hold a book the right way up. _____
- Turns pages properly. _____
- Knows that stories have a name or title. _____
- Asks for a particular story. _____
- Retells a story told to him. _____
- Shares a story or rhyme with you. _____
- Asks questions about the story. _____
- Knows that some stories begin 'Once upon a time . . . '. _____
- Points or looks to the left of a page. _____
- Knows what letters and words are. _____
- Knows that there are spaces between words. _____
- Can identify words he knows. _____
- Guesses what might happen next in a story. _____
- Can pretend to be one of the characters in a story. _____
- Points to, or identifies, his name, food labels or signs. _____
- Knows the names of favourite TV programmes. _____
- Watches you read or wants to know what you're reading. _____

Beginner

- Can identify most lower case letters. _____
- Knows how to put some vowels together to make a new sound. _____

- Knows how to put some consonants together such as 'ch' or 'dr'.   _____

- Knows how to sound vowel consonant combinations such as 'ti'/'it'.   _____

- Can identify most upper case letters.   _____

- Can read some two letter words.   _____

- Can read some three letter words.   _____

(Record the specific letters and letter combinations when your child has learned them. Use the record sheet in Figure 12 – or an adaptation of it.)

- Can identify several four or more letter words on sight.   _____

- Can use letter cards to form simple words.   _____

- Can use letter cards to make a word into a new word such as 'hop' into 'top' or 'pop'.   _____

- Knows some double syllable words.   _____

- Knows some multi-syllable words.   _____

- Reads food packets or street signs.   _____

- Can describe what happens in a story and give an opinion.   _____

- Can predict what might happen next, or the ending, in a story.   _____

- Can read basic texts aloud or silently.   _____

- Begins to show an interest in facts and non-fiction.   _____

- Enjoys sharing books with you.   _____

- Is sensitive to the story – including laughing at something funny, being a little sad at the sad parts.   _____

- Has particular reading or story preferences.   _____

- Asks questions about the text being read.   _____

Post-beginner

- Has gained fluency in reading simple text.   _____

- Reads fast enough to hear a rhyme he is saying.   _____

- Reads with some expression – emphasising certain words.   _____

- Can read silently with sustained concentration.   _____

- Can read aloud with confidence.   _____

- Can recall a story and give accurate details.   _____

- Likes books and wants to read.   _____

- Enjoys going to the library.   _____

- Has some understanding about plot and story structure.   _____

- Knows a wide range of single and multi-syllable words.   _____

- Can infer information from the text when it is not explicit. _____

- Begins to appreciate nuances and hidden meanings.   _____

- Makes up own stories or rhymes or changes familiar ones.   _____

CASE STUDIES

Mary and Sophie get an ice cream

'Come on Sophie. Let's go.'

Sophie stamped her foot defiantly. 'Don't want to!'

'Come on Sophie,' Mary sighed – realising that she should have spent more time with her daughter over the last two weeks but stock-taking at work had been so hectic and all consuming.

Mary decided on a touch of bribery. 'Look, I'll tell you what, we'll stop for an ice cream at Scrabbles on the way to the park, okay?'

'Can I have a chocolate walnut fudge?'

'Sure you can. I might even have one myself. Ready then?'

'Well, alright,' said Sophie, with caution but already imagining the cold and creamy feast awaiting her. A few moments later they were out the front door and in the street.

At that point Mary remembered that not only had she not spent enough time recently with Sophie but she'd also neglected her daughter's reading.

c	t	s (crossed out)	e	c	j	f
h	a	Knows a two letter 'o' word like on	Asks for particular stories	d	l	u
Knows a three letter 'a' word like hat	y	C	i	w (crossed out)	Knows a two letter 'i' word like in	g
b (crossed out)	v	Can predict what might happen next in a story	p	n	m	k

1. Mark through the box when your child can identify the letter or word or can do the action.
2. Leave q, x, z, till later.
3. Some two and three letter words will become familiar to your child from seeing them regularly. Present new ones, through games, in conjunction with the vocabulary list on page 128, when your child can identify some constituent sounds.

Fig. 12. Example record sheet for beginners

Uhm, she thought, too late to go back for a storybook now but maybe a game. That would be nice.

And so began a game of I-Spy that lasted the whole afternoon and well into the evening. From ordinary things to funny things. From things they saw to things they didn't, like zebras and dinosaurs. Of course, it also included ice cream.

Sam's learning takes a dive

It was 4.30, all the children had gone home and the classroom was quiet. Miss Kenford sat at her desk marking papers. As Tracy entered, she looked up.

'Good afternoon,' said Tracy, 'I'm Sam's mum. We spoke on the phone.'

'Oh, yes. Please have a seat.' Miss Kenford motioned towards the spare chair.

Removing her glasses, Miss Kenford began. 'As we discussed, I'm really concerned about Sam. He doesn't seem to be doing very well this term and considering the glowing report from last year's work, I think he's beginning to slack. In fact, he has a problem paying attention in class and I've caught him fighting in the playground a couple of times. Now I'm a great believer in teaching reading and giving the children lots of material to look at but I would say that Sam is about six months behind the rest of the children in the class. I wouldn't have called you in today but I feel that this is a problem we must nip in the bud before it has any lasting effect on Sam's education.'

Tracy looked thoughtful – she'd had a feeling something like this was coming and was prepared. 'What exactly do you think the cause of the problem is?'

'Difficult to say.' Miss Kenford smiled sweetly, 'I was hoping maybe you could enlighten me?'

'I'm afraid it's got me beat as well. But it's the reading I'm particularly concerned about. Do you have any suggestions about how to help?'

'Well, the modern approaches are the best and it's what I use here in class. Books – any type, any kind, the more the better. Children need hands-on experience of real books so that they can get used to the words.'

Tracy probed, 'What about teaching how letters fit together to make sounds? Do you think that's a good idea? I remember I learnt that way as a child.'

'Oh, education's come a long way since then. A little bit of that, perhaps, but children need room to experiment. With my methods, they're almost learning on their own.'

Tracy had heard enough. It was clear that Sam was doing badly because he wasn't getting the chance to learn. As good as modern teaching methods were, a balance of approaches was required and Sam needed instruction – which for some inexplicable reason Miss Kenford didn't seem to realise.

Kevin falls behind even though he's bright

Bill held up the report card in front of Mr Watson, the headmaster. 'If he's so intelligent, as that expensive assessment we had done said, why has he got such a lousy school report?'

Mr Watson sighed as he looked at Bill and Anne Fenton in an understanding manner. He'd seen the problem many times before during his career. 'Look, it's like this, the assessment is a good one – there's no doubt that Kevin is intelligent, in fact, above average intelligence. But the school report does show that he's fallen behind. This, unfortunately, sometimes happens with bright children.'

'But why?' said Anne.

'A number of reasons. For example, he doesn't want to show that he can do better than his friends, the work is too easy for him – so he doesn't do it. Maybe he's having problems in one area which is holding him back in all the others, or perhaps he's not relating well to his class teacher.'

Bill had calmed down somewhat but was also held in his seat, should he jump up again, by the firm grip Anne had on his arm. 'So what can we do?' he asked.

'Leave it with me,' replied Mr Watson, 'I'll look into it and find out exactly what the problem is. Then we'll see the best way to take steps to remedy the situation – perhaps Kevin just needs a bit of extra support in class.'

POINTS FOR DISCUSSION

1. You are aware that your child is developing particular hobbies and interests. How would you go about using these as a means to further her reading?

2. What interesting and entertaining places can you think of, where you
    and your child can go together?

3. What unique characteristics does your child have that will affect how
    reading development progresses?

Studying For A Degree

How to succeed as a mature student in higher education

Stephen Wade

If you are an aspiring student in adult education, or a mature learner looking for a higher education course leading to a degree, this book is specially for you. It will lead you through the academic maze of entry procedures, study programmes and teaching methods. It explains how to apply and how to contact the professionals who will help; how to survive tutorials, seminars and presentations, and how to manage your time, plan your study, and find the right support when you need it. There are sections on the credit award system, pathway planning, and useful case studies of typical students in this context.Stephen Wade PhD has 20 years' professional experience in further and higher education, and is a Course Leader for a degree programme.

£8.99, 128pp illus. paperback, 1 85703 415 5.

How To Books Ltd, Plymbridge House, Estover Road, Plymouth PL6 7PZ, United Kingdom. Tel: (01752) 202301. Fax: (01752) 202331. Please add postage & packing (£1 UK, £2 Europe, £3 world airmail).

Credit card orders may be faxed or phoned.

6
Troubleshooting Common Problems

MANAGING THE UNWILLING CHILD

Listed in this section are a variety of easily dealt with problems that affect how children learn to read.

> **I spend a small fortune on books and materials for my six-year-old but it doesn't seem to interest her.**

Consider what is actually motivating your child and ask yourself whether:

- The items you are buying are of greater interest to you than to her. If this is the case, try and find out what your child's interests really are and buy accordingly.

- The books you are buying are too sophisticated and your child cannot cope with them. Or, alternatively, they are too easy – although this is less likely to be the case.

- You may be buying too many items and your child is spoilt for choice. She may also have the idea that you're always buying these things, whether she wants them or not, and they're not really anything to do with her anyway!

- If your child's lack of interest in the books and toys you buy has developed suddenly, it is possible something is worrying her. Talk to her and if necessary the class teacher to try and find out. Keep in mind that some children bottle up worry and it only displays itself in their behaviour.

Learning to appreciate

The appreciation of a child does not come with the buying of quantity. It is important, therefore, that she is aware of the value of an item because of what it *is*, as well as what it cost – and that it's not something that's going to be bought everyday.

Think about:

* How you treat your own things. Do you value them or do you consider most things to be disposable? To some extent, most children will take after their parents!

My child hates reading and refuses to even look at a book.

This is a situation where something has turned your child right off reading. The reason may be simple or it may be more complex.

At the simple level

* He doesn't like to read because he gets nothing out of it and doesn't enjoy stories – some children get this way even though they may have been developing excellent reading skills. Sometimes it is best to do nothing for a while as the situation corrects itself. Your child may eventually realise that books are not so bad after all – trying to help may only make matters worse. If the problem does persist, try reorientating your child by suggesting different types of stories or non-fiction books that he may not have come across before.

* Your child may have gone off reading because another interest has taken over, such as computer games. In this case let him read magazines or comics associated with his specific interest. You can even make an activity out of the computer game by reading the instruction leaflet together.

* It's possible that your child's friends are influencing him. It's become 'fashionable' to dislike reading. Talk to your child, find out. Sometimes at the root of this is a ringleader who cannot read well himself and is passing on his *attitude* to other children at school.

At a more complex level

* The reason may be to do with your child's confidence and how he is

coping at school. How he gets on with the teacher as well as the teaching methods used may also influence his liking for books and reading. Talk to the school, find out what is happening. You will then be able to decide how best to help alongside the school.

- If the problem has been in evidence for some considerable time and you also know that reading skills expected for your child's age have not been reached, it could indicate a remedial problem. Again, talk to the school, find out what is happening. If you are not satisfied with the response, begin to look for alternative professional help.

> **My child only likes watching TV and films and will never listen to a story from me.**

There is nothing intrinsically wrong with liking TV and films. The real problem is if your child is using this outlet at the expense of literacy.

- It could be that your child is developing his interests within the visual arts and media rather than in book-based pursuits. This is fine and he should be given every encouragement. However, it must still be balanced with a broad literacy education.

Assuming that your child just needs 'switching on' to books then you need to find ways to interest and motivate – getting him away from a sole interest towards a more wholesome appreciation of a variety of interests.

Encouraging an interest in books

For example, you could:

(a) Use a story that is similar in type or style to those he is watching (if he likes Westerns then use Westerns). Sometimes it's possible to get books or stories by the same author on which a film was based. This can be a very good starting point for promoting interest. Rudyard Kipling's *Jungle Book* is just one famous example; the author wrote a variety of other children's stories as well (see Further Reading).

(b) Be kind but firm. If you want to read a particular story then don't get thwarted when your child obstinately refuses. Try saying something like: 'Before we have supper, I have a really interesting story to tell you.' If his face drops say: 'It's a little story and will only take two minutes.' (If it is a longer story tell a bit of it, to whet your child's appetite, and leave the rest for another time.)

(c) Consider whether in the past you have used the TV as a 'babysitter' to keep your child quiet so that you can carry on with whatever you were doing. If this is the case, the job is slightly harder but not impossible. Just start by spending a little more time communicating with your child to find out what interests him, then move on to implementing some of the ideas that have been outlined.

My child will not sit still for any length of time.

Tackling boredom

Some children get bored very quickly with what they are engaged in. They display this boredom by fidgeting and shifting around in their seat. Any activities that you do should take this into account. So maintain interest and keep up the pace by not spending too much time on any one particular activity – whether it's a story or a non-book activity. Whatever you do, be firm but don't lose your patience, it's usually not something a child can help. Generally, as children get older their tolerance increases and this type of behaviour decreases.

Hyperactivity

If your child can't keep still whatever he is doing – not just when doing an activity together with you – he might be hyperactive. Children with this problem often display annoying, repetitive and impulsive behaviour, such as knocking or banging objects, as well as excessive and inappropriate running around the house (although normal children sometimes do these things as well). If you suspect hyperactivity, ask your GP to give your child a medical check-up. Also visit a dietitian as the problem can be caused by certain dietary substances, such as food colourings and additives.

Using positive discipline

In the cultural climate of today's world, many parents give their children a great deal of freedom. This is as it should be – we do not want to return to the Victorian age, where children were seen and not heard. But children cannot always make decisions in their own best interests – given the choice, many children would eat crisps and play Nintendo all day. So parents should always be prepared to impose some level of authority. This is not intended to stifle children's inclinations but rather to help them become more aware and well-balanced.

Positive discipline is about:

- Saying no, and meaning no (or saying yes, and meaning yes) when that's your decision about a particular matter.

- Being kind, fair and firm and gaining your child's respect, as well as giving it.

- Imposing your authority when it's necessary – and *only* when it's necessary.

- The right amount of discipline to make your child a better person – it's not about corporal punishment and it's certainly not about giving you pleasure or relief!

In the context of this book, positive discipline often means being firm, when appropriate, in order to ensure that your child gains the maximum benefit possible from the activities you have chosen to do. Sometimes, it may even mean redoing a piece of shoddy work. And remember, being firm does not mean that you can't be kind and humorous at the same time.

> **My child will not make up his mind which hand to use for pointing at words and writing.**

Allowing him to choose

It makes no difference at all whether your child is right-handed or left-handed and it's not necessary or advisable to try and influence your young child's choice. In time, when he has developed a little more, he will make the choice himself. In fact, choice of handedness is laid down in his physical make-up.

For some children though, it is not an either/or situation. These children can do some things better with one hand and other things better with the other hand. Alternatively, some children can do several things equally well with both hands, while a few children can do all things equally well with both hands.

With some children, choice of handedness is delayed through inability to use or hold implements, such as cutlery or pencils, properly.

Being aware
Look at your child as he draws a picture and consider whether he:

- does better with one particular hand – choice of handedness is starting to be made

- could improve the way he holds the pencil. You may also find that you just need to wait till your child's grip becomes a little stronger

- keeps transferring the pencil from hand to hand – the pencil is too thick for him to get his fingers round comfortably.

> **My child seems below standard but the class teacher says there is no problem. What should I do?**

Believing in the teacher
Ask yourself whether you have faith in the teacher. Speak to the teacher to determine if your feelings are justified or not. If you believe that what the teacher says is a correct estimate of the situation then let her continue to handle your child's reading – keep an eye on things but try not to worry. Some children just take a little longer to grasp new ideas or concepts.

Going to the school
If possible, try and go to the school – even for a few moments – when your child is engaged in a lesson. This is useful because:

- It is beneficial to actually see your child working in the classroom setting. Many teachers welcome help from parents for certain activities and volunteering an hour or two can help put things into perspective.

- You can look at the physical location of your child in the class. It is often the quiet children who are positioned furthest away from the teacher because they don't need to be constantly attended to and told to carry on with their work. As a result, they may get less input from the teacher who, in addition, may believe that the child understands the material because she doesn't ask any questions – and she's also a very 'good' pupil!

- By being in the class or by talking to other parents you can find out how other children are performing. Keep in mind that you can only make a loose comparison, as every child is an individual. It will, however, give you the chance to assess whether some common ground has been learnt and understood or whether your child is totally bemused by what's going on around her in the classroom.

> **The class teacher says that my child has a learning problem. How do I know if this is correct?**

Is the teacher right?

As before, consider whether you have faith in the teacher's assessment of the situation. Most good teachers will be aware of reading deficiencies that require special attention and will intervene themselves or make arrangements for remedial help. Often this is provided within the school by specialist teachers.

Consider also the following questions:

1. Is poor performance limited to reading or is it observable in other subjects? If the problem is just in reading your child might simply need extra help at school or at home with you. If the problem is not confined to reading it may be as a result of the way the class teacher teaches or your child may have a more severe learning problem, causing her to fall behind across the board – inabilities in one subject having a knock-on effect on others.

2. Has the class teacher identified the problem early or late? And if specialist assessments are called for, have these been organised? Does the headteacher know about the problem? (After all, she will be the one who will be organising the administration for any outside specialist help).

Teachers are not always experts

Although teachers can identify poor performance and areas of educational deficiency very well, they may not always be the best people to identify a specific learning problem (which may have a medical or psychological base). The result of this is that lack of motivation, or even sheer boredom, can be wrongly labelled as a learning problem, when in fact all that is required is a change of approach. The opposite can be true as well. So that a child who does indeed have a severe learning problem, requiring specialist help, can be labelled a 'time-waster' or a child who 'must try harder'.

Assessing the situation yourself
Some things to check are:

- The general level of attainment of other children.
- The location of your child in the class.
- What books and materials are used.
- The amount of time the teacher actually spends reading with your child.
- The amount of time spent on book-based activities.

Consider also:

- The length of time that the class teacher has been teaching your child. Sometimes a new teacher, or a supply teacher, takes over. Many children are sensitive to changes of this nature – while the work of some can vary dramatically.

Varda gets informed

'I hear the new teacher for class four is settling in very well,' said Varda. Her bandaged arm was carefully positioned in a sling across her chest.

Jemma moved the pushchair to one side to get closer to speak. 'It's about time the school got its act together. I mean, those supply teachers did the best they could but five in seven months was a bit over the top. The children didn't know where they were.'

'Yes, I thought much the same thing. I haven't had the chance to meet Mrs McDonald yet, is she good?'

'She seems to be and I've noticed Damien's reading has improved slightly in the last two months, since he started bringing books home again.'

Varda frowned, 'Hmm, I didn't know they'd started reading homework again. Ahktar never said a word. I don't think he's been doing it.'

'Haven't you signed his record card?' She glanced at the bandage. 'Silly me, course you didn't. Oh, go easy on him – he probably hasn't got used to Mrs McDonald yet.'

DEALING WITH PHYSICAL PROBLEMS

The common physical problems that afflict young children are sometimes overlooked. Early diagnosis and treatment will ensure that your child's reading and education are not held back.

Childhood speech impediments

The physical make-up of your child will dictate how he uses his body. Hence, how he uses his mouth, throat and voice to produce understandable sounds. Some children have specific difficulties with this. For example, manipulating the tongue in order to articulate words clearly.

Children's speech problems include:

- **A common problem** – a young child with a lisp who says 'th' for 's'.

- **A less common problem** – continual use of a particular letter instead of the correct letter, or inability to use a particular letter, for example, 'y' instead of 'l', where a child would say 'yeyyow' for 'yellow'.

Checking things out

Whatever the impediment, if it isn't transitory – such as when teeth are coming through – but has been in evidence since you can remember, then a check-up by your GP, and possibly dentist, to ensure proper development of your child's mouth is called for. If this proves alright then your child can be referred to a speech therapist, who with specific techniques and exercises can significantly improve articulation.

Why do some parents wait so long?

Some parents get used to their child talking with an impediment, while a minority of parents think that it is cute if their child talks in an odd way. Other parents simply don't recognise that there is a problem that needs to be dealt with.

Whatever you do, don't delay in addressing the speech problem before it impacts on your child's education.

Hearing problems

Sometimes, speech problems may be caused by poor or defective hearing. Certainly, an inability to hear properly can lead to a variety of educational problems.

Assuming that your child does not suffer from profound deafness – which has already been diagnosed and the appropriate medical steps taken – then it is possible that your child's poor hearing is being caused by ear infections. Sometimes a cold is accompanied by infection, feeling unwell and earache. Depending on the reason, a high temperature can also occur. With acute or repeated ear infections the liquid that builds up in the middle ear does not have a chance to drain and can result in the condition commonly known as 'glue ear'.

If you suspect ear infection, glue ear or any other problem that could potentially harm your child's hearing, get him checked by your GP as soon as possible. The sooner treatment is started the sooner your child will be able to hear what he is being taught.

Sight problems

There are a variety of eyesight problems that can delay reading development or stop it completely. Even if vision is relatively good and the problem is minor, a child can give up after trying for a few minutes due to fatigue. After a while, an aversion to reading is produced which stops any future progress.

Common eyesight problems include:

- **Nearsightedness** − (myopia) inability to focus on distant objects.

- **Farsightedness** − inability to focus on near objects.

- **Astigmatism** − focusing distortions.

- **Squint** − eye movements don't coordinate when looking at objects.

Jessica takes a look

After popping in to the optician to collect Simon's new glasses, Jessica decided to surprise Simon and deliver them personally to him at school − not that Simon liked his new glasses but they looked good on him and just like her husband's did.

Jessica stood by the classroom door and watched her son through the little window. She noticed that Simon was sitting near the back and not taking much notice of what was going on. I think I need to have a word with Mr Newton about this, she thought. My mistake, I should have spoken to him before about Simon's nearsightedness. I'll show Mr Newton the glasses, to make sure he knows Simon's supposed to wear them, and ask him if he can change Simon's seat to one closer to the front.

IDENTIFYING DYSLEXIA

Dyslexia and related disorders affect about one in ten people and about four times as many boys than girls. It has nothing to do with intelligence. In fact, some very famous and intelligent people are believed to have been dyslexic. These include Einstein, Leonardo da Vinci and Thomas Edison.

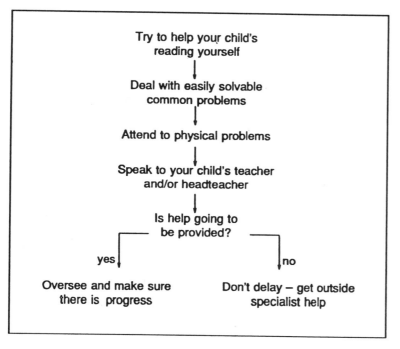

Fig. 13. Dealing with problems.

Dyslexia – what is it?

The term dyslexic is applied to a child who has significant difficulty in learning to read – or fails to learn to read – where there is no evidence of brain damage, mental retardation, severe emotional problems or cultural factors such as coming from a home where the national language is not spoken. In other words, all other factors that could delay reading development must be ruled out. This leaves some sort of underlying perceptual or higher mental function that is not working correctly.

Characteristics of dyslexia include:

- Difficulty in distinguishing the use of right and left hands.
- 'Seeing' letters back to front, or not at all, which causes confusion.
- Leaving out or putting in words when reading.
- Confusing small words such as: of, for, from.
- Guessing long words.

- Monotonous tone when reading aloud.
- Difficulty carrying out three instructions in sequence.
- Having another family member with similar difficulties.

Dyslexia is still a mystery

The problem with dyslexia is that it is very hard to characterise. Precisely what perceptual abilities are not working correctly and how bad does reading have to be before it is classified as dyslexia? We are not yet at the stage where we understand the workings of the brain sufficiently well to be able to decide exactly what is going on. It does seem to be the case though, that dyslexia, with all its associated characteristics, is a symptom rather than a specific cause – just as a child can have measles but what you see is the fever and the rash.

The problem with diagnosing dyslexia

Because of the lack of agreement between educators, psychologists and doctors as to precisely what underlies dyslexia:

A. Some teachers might wrongly label a child as dyslexic before they have tried different avenues of approach to help reading.

B. A child who is dyslexic may be diagnosed late or not at all.

The solution

There is no magic cure for dyslexia. Development of reading ability is by sitting with a teacher or specialist who can devote sufficient time to provide the necessary remedial help. However, in a minority of instances, favourable claims have been made for the use of coloured spectacles while learning.

Attention deficit disorder

This problem is similar to hyperactivity but is believed to have its origins in the way information is transmitted across nerve connections at the front of the brain. Like dyslexia, ADD is believed to be inherited.

ADD can be easily misdiagnosed − as the behaviours displayed can suggest other disorders or can be taken to be a simple educational problem. Children with ADD might also be dyslexic.

Characteristics of ADD include:

- lack of attention
- lack of motivation
- fidgeting or inability to sit still
- forgetting
- taking overly long to complete tasks or meals
- daydreaming
- irritability
- sudden drops in school performance.
- impulsive actions
- disruptive behaviour

The solution

There is no medical cure − although drugs, such as Ritalin are used in severe cases. The problem is dealt with by combining your efforts with that of the school and a psychologist who should be brought in to help.

The advice given will be in order to structure your child's learning so that tasks become easier. As backup to this, positive discipline is stressed using specific instructions. For example:

- We always clear the plate away after we've eaten.

- When we've used the toothpaste, we put the cap back on.

- We put the comics back in the pile after we've read them.

COPING WITH ILLNESS AND READING DEVELOPMENT

Illness of any kind is going to impact on your child's education. The extent of the impact will depend on the severity of the illness and whether it is short term or long term.

Short-term illness
Where there are no significant after-effects, a child will normally be able to make up any lost educational ground. She may, however, require some extra help to get her going again.

Long-term illness
A child's energies are going to be geared towards lack of health, feeling unwell and dealing with any uncomfortable treatments that she may receive. Even if she seems to be coping well, at a subconscious level a significant amount of mental energy will be devoted to survival and day-to-day problems that the illness produces. It is inevitable, therefore, that reading development and general education will suffer.

Maintaining reading
There are no easy answers if your child is in this position. The prime concern, of course, is to get her better. But if your child can read a little on her own or you are able to help her reading along with some pleasant learning sessions – such as reading to her or reading together some easy books or comics – then there is a far greater chance that her reading will develop, even if it takes longer. As an added bonus, when she does recover, there is a greater chance of achieving success in other subjects because she will be able to read for herself.

Keep overseeing
Obviously, the age at which the illness occurs will have a bearing on the level of ability reached. However, mainstream schools are not usually geared towards the child who is constantly away and as a child gets older this becomes more of an issue as the pace of education increases. You can do a great deal though, simply by:

(a) providing interesting and exciting reading material
(b) letting your child develop her abilities and interests at her own pace.

Whatever you do, *go easy* and don't transfer your fears about your child's education to her and make what should be a fun outlet and diversion into a chore and something to be avoided.

SEEKING OUTSIDE HELP

Your child's school is the first place to go to talk about your concerns. Many schools have teachers with specific remedial education skills who run special classes to give children the extra push that they may need. If necessary, find out who this person is and what you can do to help matters along.

If no appropriate help is available – as might be the case in some independent schools – you will need to consider the extent to which you are able to:

- help matters yourself
- employ private tutors or specialists
- change schools.

Psychological assessment

When problems require more expert attention, the school will often work with the Local Education Authority and specialists who can assess, advise and structure a special curriculum for your child. Sometimes, this forms part of what is known as the **statementing procedure** – which is a statement of **Special Educational Needs (SEN)**. This allows for outside specialist teachers or helpers to come into the school for a certain number of hours to help with educational or psychological problems. There is also provision for attending special schools.

The statementing procedure

The statementing procedure is useful but it has limitations. It can, for example, be drawn out. By the time the appropriate help is obtained, key moments in your child's educational life may have passed. There is also little provision for those children who are on the boundary of special educational needs – as there is little provision for those children who are above average ability and are educationally gifted.

Getting expert advice and help

Although sometimes parents need to push to make sure their child is given the help they need, most good schools will be aware, before you, of your child's educational problems and will organise accordingly. You can, however, approach:

- Your Local Education Authority for guidance.

Father's legal battle to help dyslexic pupil

By ALISON BRACE
Education Correspondent

A TEN-YEAR-OLD boy with dyslexia has been barred from attending a private school by a local authority.

Lester Bowen's father was set to pay £7,500 a year to help his son overcome reading problems.

But Trafford council in Greater Manchester took Kevin Bowen to court saying Lester did not have dyslexia but did have learning problems best tackled in the State system.

The council won and Lester, from Sale, Cheshire, has returned to a school for children with special needs instead of going to the preparatory school he wanted to attend.

Now Mr Bowen, a builder, hopes to challenge the ruling in the High Court, claiming the authority's officers and psychologists acted unreasonably. He claims they ignored two independent assessments which stated that Lester was dyslexic.

Judge

Mr Bowen also says they took more than two years to issue a statement of his special needs.

After the boy's reading failed to improve at the State school, Mr Bowen enrolled him at private Ramillies Hall school, in Cheadle Hulme, which provides for pupils with learning difficulties.

After advice from independent experts a judge ruled in June that Lester should attend Ramillies Hall.

Child psychologist Dr Harry Chasty criticised the authority's diagnosis of Lester's problems as 'inaccurate' and said the State school was unsuitable.

But Trafford education chiefs said the school would not fulfil Lester's needs — and stopped him going.

Mr Bowen said: 'I hope to challenge Trafford on the basis that they are being utterly unreasonable.'

Trafford council refused to comment.

The Mail on Sunday, October 16, 1994

Fig. 14. Assessments should be to help children.

Reproduced by permission of *The Mail on Sunday.*

- Your GP, who may refer your child to a Learning Difficulties Clinic.

- Independent educational psychologists who can carry out private assessments.

Employing professional tutors

Often, all that is required – even in quite difficult situations – is support by somebody who is emotionally unconnected to your child's reading problem – you might be too close due to your concern over your child's future progress.

Finding a tutor

Many school teachers also work part time, on a private basis, and do an extremely worthwhile job. They can be found through:

- recommendation from other parents
- tutorial agencies
- the local press.

In most cases, it is best to avoid using the same teacher as the one who teaches your child in school because:

- If your child is falling behind they should be helped by this particular teacher *during* school time (or provision made within the school).

- As the old saying goes, 'Variety is the spice of life'. A different teacher can bring a different and fresh perspective to your child's needs.

Tutors come from many walks

There are some individuals who teach privately but who may not be school teachers. Graduates with high qualifications, for example, often do this and can be extremely good at the job. The reasons for this include:

(a) They may have a greater understanding of the learning process as they have experienced it themselves fairly recently.

(b) They are not hidebound by educational theories which can dictate teaching practice.

(c) Although it is a means of gaining a livelihood, many of these individuals enjoy their work and can pass on their enthusiasm to their pupils.

Qualifications to look for
On the basis of what has been said, the minimum qualifications you should be looking for in a tutor are a degree, or its equivalent, and/or a teaching qualification.

Getting a good tutor
When you hire a tutor, you will need to satisfy yourself that the person can actually help. The first lesson should provide a basic assessment of your child's needs and you should have a chance to discuss this afterwards. During the lesson, it is best to let the teacher get on with teaching and not to hover around – as you are likely to put your child off as well as the teacher. If you are concerned about leaving your child alone then leave the door open so that you can hear what is going on.

Remember that it may take several lessons before your child settles into learning properly. As when carrying out a learning session yourself, it is normally advisable to have the teacher provide lessons two or three times a week. Although the cost is higher, your child is likely to learn that much faster.

CASE STUDIES

Sophie catches a cold
The snivels turned to sneezes and the sneezes turned into a high temperature and fever. The doctor was called, said that all would be well in a few days, and quickly left.

It took a full three weeks for Sophie to get back to her former energetic self, during which time it seemed that her classmates had forged ahead.

'Don't worry about a thing,' said the headmaster to Mary on the morning Sophie returned to school. 'Sophie's missed a lot but she can soon make it up. I've already discussed the matter with Miss Dempsy and Sophie will be given all the help she needs to get her back up to standard. She was doing so well before and we don't want her to lose any of the headway she's made. If necessary, we can also organise some extra remedial help.'

All the support had the desired effect and Sophie's reading was soon back on track.

How Tracy found that Sam was dyslexic
Tracy thought long and hard before employing a tutor but there didn't

seem to be any alternative. Sam was not doing well at school – partly due to Miss Kenford's methods – and there were limitations to what Tracy herself could do. It seemed that Sam would learn for a while but it would only go so far and he'd keep making the same mistakes, over and over again – as if he'd come to a wall and could go no further.

'Well, how did Sam do?' she asked Brian Taylor after he'd completed the first lesson.

Brian looked thoughtful and then replied, 'Sam tried really hard but it's incredibly difficult for him. This needs confirming by a psychologist but you do know, I suppose, that it's possible he's dyslexic.'

'No, I had no idea! His school never said a word.'

'That's the reason why his reading has come to a standstill. He's making all the classic mistakes – saying words that aren't there, confusing letters and so forth. I wouldn't blame anybody for not having noticed it previously; it's only now, as he's a little bit older, that the problem is more apparent.'

'Will he be alright? Is there anything I should do?'

'Certainly the school should know at some point and they may want to organise an assessment and provide more specialist help. But, in the meantime, I'll work with him and we'll see how far we can go. With some one-to-one tuition, he stands a good chance of progressing.'

Kevin returns to school

Everyone was pleased to see Kevin back at school after being in hospital for six months; from Mr Watson, the headmaster, to Nora Norden, the dinner lady, who gave him an extra special helping of chocolate pudding. But, it soon became clear how much work Kevin had missed.

After a few days the reasons why Kevin had been away seemed to have been forgotten and Kevin was told things like, 'Come on, try a bit harder, otherwise you won't catch up.' And 'You're not doing very well, Kevin. You don't want to have to stay down a year, do you?' This all made Kevin very depressed and within a few weeks he was hating it, and didn't want to go to school in the mornings anymore. There'd be arguments, tears and complaints of feeling ill before finally getting him ready and on his way.

Bill and Anne could see what the problem was and decided to have a good talk with Mr Watson. 'After all,' Bill said to him, 'surely you realise how hard it's been for Kevin. Why didn't you organise some special lessons as back up to his classwork?'

'You're right,' said Mr Watson, swallowing hard. 'We've been extremely remiss and unfeeling in this situation. Although it's no excuse, part of the reason has been the amount of time spent recently on National Curriculum assessments by the teachers here. I can only apologise and say that we will be more sensitive to Kevin's needs in the future and that remedial support will be organised – even if I have to teach Kevin myself.'

POINTS FOR DISCUSSION

1. How would you deal with the situation if your child decided he didn't like books anymore?

2. In what circumstances, when you're trying to teach reading, would positive discipline be useful?

3. What is the value in dealing early on with physical problems or dyslexia?

7
Preparing for the Information Age

SHARING LEARNING OPPORTUNITIES

Throughout this book information has been provided about how to help your child to read – formally, informally, when there are problems, and so on. But all this doesn't happen in a vacuum. The society and culture in which you live plays a big part – how you prepare your child for the future, how you teach your child, and how you share with your child are directly related to this.

Building for the future

To prepare your child for a fast moving, technological world – and help her to succeed – think about how the following points reflect your ability to share together and how they will affect your child's reading development:

1. Is your child taught differently to how you were as a child because of technological change?

2. What pressures are there on your family – financial, single parenting, time, lifestyle, and so on?

3. What does sharing mean in a 'me' society – a society in which people often put themselves before others? Is our society like this and if it is, how do you really share effective learning opportunities with your child?

4. What values are important in today's world – old values, new values, family values? Does reading and telling stories give over these values?

5. Will the information age be useful to your child?

6. Has your child's work or career expectation changed as a result of technology? And is this reflected in what she reads?

7. Is it possible to be illiterate when we are surrounded by words – newspapers, computers, hoardings, books, packaging, and so on?

Sharing for success
The information age is here to stay – there's no doubt about that. But, whatever your feelings are about the above points, technology is like the proverbial double edged sword – it can be used for bad or good – it's up to the user. So, when you are out and about with your child or choosing books or materials, remember that your responsibility includes:

● Ensuring that your child gains the necessary confidence to be able to tackle the world of tomorrow and has the reading and educational skills to achieve it.

● Giving over important values that will help your child live life successfully in the future.

In this way you are not just sharing books and stories but also your own unique knowledge and experience.

MEETING THE DEMANDS OF TODAY

Reading skills must be passed on but it's not always as simple as teaching 'a, b, c,'. There are special demands in today's world – both in the UK and around the world – which children must meet in order to progress.
    Broadly, these are:

● technological
● educational
● social.

Data communication
Perhaps the most important thing to come out of the present information age is our ability to communicate electronically. But, interestingly, far from reducing the amount of information written down on paper, we now .seem to have vast amounts of printed material – think about the last lot of junk mail you received!

On balance though, there are many advantages to electronic communication. It is:

- safe
- reliable
- not hampered by delays
- unaffected by weather
- available over great distances.

The result of this is that important information – such as financial or medical – gets to where it's needed fast and efficiently. It is then read and used by the person who requested it, anywhere in the world. Similarly, it is now increasingly common for young children to have access to the Internet – the computerised global network, on the information superhighway – to use games and library databases.

Limiting opportunities

Whatever the reason, a child who cannot read properly is at a serious disadvantage in today's modern world. A child, though, doesn't understand this, so parents and teachers need to take responsibility for education – taking into account why reading may be delayed – and prepare the child adequately for the demands ahead.

The importance of reading skills
Without good reading skills, a child will have difficulty:

- learning
- communicating
- in future education
- getting a job or career
- using sophisticated technology.

At a young age, a child may not be aware of the full consequences of his lack of ability but he will be aware of it compared with other children. If his friends are forging ahead and he isn't then his self-image and confidence are going to take a beating. He might try a bit of bravado and pretend that it doesn't really matter but deep down he will be aware of a certain inadequency. As he gets older, unless there is significant improvement, this feeling is likely to increase.

Reading is everyone's concern

When a child who cannot read properly is part of a group of children who also have poor reading skills and tend to despise reading and education, each reinforcing the other, then who can predict what the full social consequences can be? Needless to say, these children are not being given the best possible chance to succeed in life.

Reading and power

In developing countries such as those in Africa or South America, reading issues have a much wider impact than in Western countries because lack of reading ability is far more widespread. Currently, efforts are made by organisations like Unesco to teach mothers because it is believed that mothers are the key to social change. It is the way to bring these countries into the information age.

By teaching mothers to read there will be:

- more daughters and sons learning to read
- greater access to healthcare including pre-natal information and care
- higher personal status
- better quality farming
- greater job opportunities.

Making reading a priority

In the UK standards in the last 20 years appear to have dropped significantly. A recent report by the Adult Literacy and Basic Skills Unit suggested that, in the 22 to 24 age group, around half of those surveyed were below average – having trouble reading newspapers or magazines – and 20 per cent had difficulty with forms at work. For the world of tomorrow to be better than the world of today, these trends must be reversed.

The fact is that whether a child is in a rural town in Mali or an inner-city area in the middle of London, it really doesn't matter. The functioning of a modern, healthy society rests on basic skills – and reading is one of them.

READING THE FUTURE

The education of your child is your overall responsibility. Not just because you want to ensure that your child does well in reading and gets a good job but because how we teach children dictates how our society develops. To an extent, as a parent, this is in your hands. So give careful thought to what your child is learning at school and what she is learning at home with you. What you put in, you are likely to eventually get out!

Getting ready for tomorrow

It is a technological world that we live in and your child is ideally placed to make use of computers and all the marvellous mechanisms that make life a little bit easier. Whatever is invented though – and who knows what the next fantastic, scientific breakthrough will bring – the ability to read and make sense of somebody else's ideas on paper, or in an electronic medium, is always going to be of prime importance, at home or in the workplace.

Reading is not only about the expression of ideas but, as mentioned early on in this book, it is about communication. There will always be a demand for this as it is a way of passing on Man's cultural inheritance to future generations. Reading, therefore, is *essential* – but it is also *enjoyable*.

CASE STUDIES

Sophie at 18

The kitchen door burst open and Sophie rushed in to where her parents and older sister were sitting eating breakfast. 'I've passed! I've passed! I've passed all my exams!'

'Well done!' cried Mary, before all the others joined in. The family gathered around her, all talking at the same time and all eager to have a look at the little slip of paper that meant so much.

Sophie's father finally managed to get a word in. 'So, have you decided what your next step is?'

'Yes, Dad. I think I'm going to take that offer of a university place to study computer engineering. Looks like I'm going to follow in your footsteps after all.'

Sam at 25

'So, what do you think, Mum? You reckon I deserved the award?'

Tracy examined the framed picture of a complicated component, holding it carefully in her hands.

'Yes, Sam. You most certainly deserved the award. There aren't many designers in the aerospace industry who could have produced a design like this – and certainly none who could have done it in such a beautiful way.'

'Aw, you're just saying that,' Sam teased.

'You think so, eh young man? I was just thinking. Do you remember your first tutor, Brian Taylor?'

'Sure. What about him?'

'When he told me you were dyslexic, it was like falling through the floor. I didn't know what to do. But then a few weeks after he started working with you, he said that you were good at drawing and he told me also that dyslexic people are often good at draughting and designing. We decided to see if we could help you along with this. And slowly, over the years, your talents developed. So, Sam, when I say it's beautiful, I mean it's beautiful! Okay?'

Sam laughed, 'Alright Mum, no arguments, whatever you say. Now, can I take you out to celebrate?'

Kevin at 22

Bill and Anne held hands as the new sign went up above the shop. It read: **Fenton and Son, The Home of Fine Furniture.**

'Not bad, is it Dad?' Kevin came out from the new shop premises wearing the latest business suit.

'You know, son. When you left school early, I was worried – even though you seemed so sure that travelling around the world was what you wanted to do. But in my wildest dreams, I never expected you to succeed so quickly.'

'Well, I can't say that I ever really enjoyed school. Although they did try very hard to help me get somewhere, especially old Mr Watson. But I was never what you'd call academically inclined. Really, it was down to you and Mum. You never forced me into a career that I didn't want but you always kept me interested in books and there was always something to read. That's what got me interested in travelling – those marvellous books about the Himalayas and the Asian jungles. Those and other books also gave me the ideas about how to develop our business, importing foreign, quality furniture.'

Bill smiled broadly as he put his free arm around Kevin's shoulder, 'I guess we did something right after all then?'

'Oh, I don't know,' laughed Kevin, 'the computer you bought is still not producing the correct invoices. I reckon Mum's going to have to help you again with that one!'

POINTS FOR DISCUSSION

1. What skills or abilities don't you have – but think you could get – that would help you and your child make better use of the technology of the information age?

2. Do you think that all or only some of the things your child learns at school will be useful in years to come?

3. Where do you see your child in 15 years' time? Do you think your child is prepared for the demands ahead, both in reading and in other subjects?

Simple Vocabulary

VOWEL AND VOWEL COMBINATIONS

a	*e*	*i*	*o*	*u*	*ee*	*ea*
at	hen	is	to	us	see	sea
as	men	it	do	up	bee	seat
an	den	win	so	bus	peel	tea
pan	get	bit	on	cup	keen	eat
ran	set	pin	hop	fun	feel	bean
cap	wet	tin	mop	sun	been	beat
tap	met	fin	pop	mud	seen	mean
map	let	lip	top	run	feed	meat
can	bed	sip	dog	bun	heel	bead
fan	fed	pit	fog	pup	seed	heat
man	bet	tip	log	but	feet	near
bat	net	sit	hot	cut	meet	dear
cat	led	hip	rot	hut	weed	fear

128

fat	wed	did	cot	jut	beer	bear
hat	ten	hid	dot	nut	need	weak
sat	yes	lid	job	mum	seem	seam
dad	yet	big	not	sum	seed	team
lad	pet	dig	pot	bug	keep	real
mad	peg	fit	box	hug	weep	leap
pad	beg	pig	fox	mug	peek	meal
bad	pen	wig	nod	hum	leek	year
sad	egg	bin	rod	rum	deep	hear
had	jet	fig	jot	tub	peep	seal
jam	red	din	tot	cub	seep	deal

oo	*ai*	*oa*	*ou*	*oi*	*ie*
book	air	oak	out	oil	pie
look	hair	oat	about	boil	lie
cook	fair	boat	loud	foil	lied
took	pair	load	our	toil	tie
hook	paid	toad	round	coin	tied
good	said	moan	found	join	tried
wood	pail	coat	mound	coil	cried
wool	tail	road	mouth	soil	fried

food	fail	coal	sound	spoil
hood	wail	goal	bound	point
pool	rain	soap	mount	joint
cool	raid	soak	count	noise
tool	mail	loaf	mouse	voice
fool	sail	oaf	house	
room	hail	goat	shout	
foot	nail	boat	pound	
soon	maid	float	sour	
boot	gain	roast	wound	
root	main	coast	hound	

CONSONANT COMBINATIONS

ch	*st*	*th*	*br*	*sh*	*sw*
chap	stop	the	brim	she	sweep
chop	step	this	broom	shin	sweet
chain	steal	that	brow	shiny	sweat
chair	steel	they	brat	shell	swag
chart	stole	then	bran	shop	swallow
chat	street	them	brain	shut	swan
chase	still	those	brag	sheet	swap

check	post	these	bread	ship	swarm
cheat	rust	there	bride	shoot	swim
cheep	must	their	broth	shake	swing
cheek	lost	with	break	shady	swish
cheer	most	thank	brake	sharp	swirl
cheese	just	thing	braid	shall	swoop
chest	fast	thud	branch	shape	sway
child	past	think	brandy	shift	swipe
chime	last	fifth	brave	shed	swot
chick	cost	thumb	breath	shirt	sword
chin	pest	thin	brown	shock	swift
china	test	three	brick	show	swivel
chip	west	thaw	brew	sheep	swig

Final y

by	fly	cry	try	sly	sty	buy
my	dry	fry	sky	spy	guy	why

Glossary

Aphasia. A failure in language use caused by brain damage.

Attention deficit disorder (ADD). An inability to pay attention, usually accompanied by fidgeting and impulsive behaviour. Thought to be caused by incorrect brain functioning.

Child centered. An educational approach in which children develop and explore their own ideas with minimal teacher instruction.

Consonant. All the alphabet letters other than a, e, i, o, u.

Contact time. Time spent with another person.

Dysgraphia. An inability to learn to write.

Dyslexia. An inability to learn to read when all physical, emotional and social reasons have been ruled out.

Dyslogia. An inability to express ideas verbally.

Flashcards. Cards with pictures, words or letters.

Giftedness. Above average ability in a specific field.

GP (General Practitioner). Family doctor.

Hyperactivity. Inappropriate running around or fidgeting. Sometimes caused by diet. Can accompany ADD.

Information technology. The storage, manipulation and movement of information through computer systems.

Learning session. Learning formally or informally in a variety of settings.

Look and say. An approach stressing whole word recognition activities.

National Curriculum. A national syllabus and assessment procedure for all UK children.

Phonics. An approach stressing the sounding of letters and letter groups.

Positive discipline. Being fair, firm and using appropriate rules to develop sensitivity, awareness and educational ability.

Psychiatrist. A medically qualified doctor specialising in the treatment of mental and psychological disorders.

Psychologist. An academically qualified practitioner specialising in the treatment of behavioural and psychological disorders. The two types relevant to children are – educational psychologists (school psychologists in the USA) and clinical psychologists.

Psychometric test. A paper and pencil or computerised test used by psychologists for assessment.

Reading ages. A method of testing reading standard based on what groups of children can do at a certain age.

Reading scheme. A set of books graded in difficulty.

Reading system. The method of sending books home with children for homework.

Real books. Ordinary books that are not part of any reading scheme.

Remedial support. Extra help in reading or other subjects according to individual needs.

Sibling. A person's brother or sister.

Special education. A structured learning program based on the assessment of a child's specific education needs.

Specific learning disability (SLD). An umbrella term for problems such as dysgraphia and dyslexia.

Speech therapist. A person who specialises in correcting speech defects.

Statementing. Statement of special educational needs (SEN) for children requiring specialist educational or psychological support.

Three Rs (3Rs). Popular term for reading, writing and arithmetic.

Vowel. The letters – a, e, i, o, u.

Further Reading

SELECTED READING FOR CHILDREN UNDER SEVEN

a is for apple (Ladybird).
Elmer The Elephant, David Mckee (Red Fox).
Poems for Seven Year Olds and Under, Helen Nicoll (ed) (Puffin).
Hot Dog and Other Poems, Kit Wright (Puffin).
Puffin Book of Nursery Rhymes (Puffin).
Each Peach, Pear, Plum, Janet and Allan Ahlberg (Kestrel).
Winnie The Pooh, A A Milne (Dean).
The Very Hungry Caterpillar, Eric Carle (Puffin).
A Fly Went By, Mike McClintock (Collins).
Little Grey Rabbit stories, Allison Uttley (Collins).
The Cat in the Hat (and other books), Dr Seuss (Collins).
A Dark, Dark Tale, Ruth Brown (Red Fox).
The Berenstein Bears and The Spooky Old Tree, Stan and Jan Berenstein
    (Collins).
The Just So Stories, Rudyard Kipling (Macmillan).
The Tale of Peter Rabbit, Beatrix Potter (Warne).
The Iron Man, Ted Hughes (Faber).
Little Bear books, Elsa Holmelund Minarik (Mammoth).
Necklace of Raindrops, Joan Aitken (Puffin).
Stanley the Caveman, Syd Hoff (Heinemann).
My Cat Likes to Hide in Boxes, Eve Sutton and Lynley Dodd (Puffin).
We're Going On A Bear Hunt, Michael Rosen (Walker Books).
Conker, Barrie Watts (Stopwatch).
Frog and Toad stories, Arnold Lobel (Puffin).
Lady Daisy, Dick King-Smith (Penguin).
Dogger, Shirley Hughes (Red Fox).

Note: Many of these books are available from more than one publisher.

Index

HOW TO BE AN EFFECTIVE SCHOOL GOVERNOR
A practical handbook for parents
Polly Bird

A revised and updated new edition of a practical beginner's guide. 'The most sensible guide to the role of the school governor that I have read ... All schools should have copies for existing and potential governors.' *Ray Acton, Former Chief Adviser, Doncaster LEA*. 'A plain, jargon-free guide to all aspects of school governorship from the lay person's point of view ... an essential purchase for all school governing bodies.' *Derek Swetnam, Chairman of Governors, Staffordshire*. 'Contains a wealth of useful information and sound advice.' *Journal of the National Association of Governors and Managers*.

176pp illus. 1 85703 123 7. 2nd edition.

HOW TO CLAIM STATE BENEFITS
A practical guide for claimants and advisers
Martin Rathfelder

The Welfare State changes all the time. The third edition of this book has been completely rewritten to take full account of the abolition of the poll tax, mobility allowance, invalidity benefit and unemployment benefit, and the introduction of council tax, disability living allowance, incapacity benefit and jobseeker's allowance – as well as many minor changes. It is the only popular paperback which explains the whole range of benefits available from local and central government, showing you exactly how to claim, and how to arrange your affairs to take advantage of the current benefit system.

160pp illus. 1 85703 073 7. 3rd edition

HOW TO RAISE FUNDS & SPONSORSHIP
A complete step-by-step guide to success
Chriss McCallum

Your project needs money. Where will you get it? How? Who will help and where do you start? 'Chriss McCallum's book is a model of its kind. Everything is set out in an easy to find way. Not a word is wasted and the advice is extremely sensible. I cannot recommend it too highly.' *The Woman Journalist*. 'Takes you step-by-step from the very beginning ... Includes some very important information such as the law around lotteries and flag days.' *Voluntary Voice*. 'The definitive work on fund raising, and virtually essential for anybody who is involved in such ventures, particularly those starting from scratch.' *Warrington Guardian*. 'Recommended.' *London Calling*.

156pp illus. 1 85703 037 0.